THE KOSHER Grapevine

IRVING LANGER

THE KOSHER

Grapevine

EXPLORING
THE WORLD OF
FINE WINE

INTRODUCTION BY DANIEL ROGOV, *Z"L*

gefen גפן
publishing house בית להוצאה לאור
JERUSALEM ◆ NEW YORK   Est. 1981

Contents

Preface

THE OCCASION of my sixtieth birthday released a salvo of thoughts and feelings within me. I reflected upon the Talmudic statement in Ethics of the Fathers which gives names to the decades of life. *"Ben shishim le'ziknah"* is how the Talmud refers to one who has reached the sixth decade of life. The words literally mean "At sixty, a person achieves [the level of] old age."

From my deep sense of gratitude, my recollections and contemplations, an "Aha!" moment emerged. I realized that the Jewish concept of *ziknah*, old age, is not a time of decline but rather a dynamic period of growth, development, and discovery that builds upon the wisdom of experience. To reach the milestone of sixty is to stand upon the threshold of a new vista, virtually the Youth of Old Age. Those who stand at this juncture have the privilege, indeed the obligation, to shape this future, to fill these years with energy and insight, to make them a fulfilling time for ourselves and those around us.

What an exciting time of life! Our convictions and values remain; but our opportunities and priorities may have shifted. Perhaps we have outgrown some dreams and justifiably let them go, but others may deserve a fresh focus and be more attainable. And we just might develop brand-new visions and goals. I, for one, would like to embark on a leisurely journey, revisiting what I didn't have the time or wisdom to properly appreciate in my younger years, as well as looking for some new adventures in G-d's wonderful world.

I have written this book so you can join me. But I'd like you to know about two other important people who will be with us on this journey: my dear parents. This requires a bit of explanation.

Sociologists would classify me as belonging to the "baby boomer generation," which encompasses those born between 1946 and 1964. I am sure this classification has value, but I prefer a different frame of reference. I was born in a Displaced Persons Camp in Europe, where my parents were married after they were liberated from concentration camps. I belong to the "first post-Holocaust generation."

As we mature, most people realize that, like it or not, we are more like our parents than we ever thought we would be – from values to physical characteristics, habits, and mannerisms. But if our parents are Holocaust survivors, they have lived through unspeakable horrors; they have endured things to which we cannot relate; their lives have been profoundly different from ours. Can we still talk about similarity and continuity between parents and children?

For me, the answer is a profound yes, because I believe in miracles. It is nothing short of miraculous that my parents were not left with crushed spirits and warped minds. I believe that any Holocaust survivor who manages to pursue life with some semblance of normalcy is a walking miracle. Such were my parents. Their will to live never faltered. They were determined to build a life. I know they did it, to a large extent, for the sake of my brothers and me. And part of that miracle was that they were able, by example, to impart to us an essential appreciation of life, a lesson they had learned under duress.

My generation saw our parents live every day just to survive. Life in the post-Holocaust world, in a new country with unfamiliar ways and language, bereft of family and resources, did not allow our parents an opportunity to think ahead and make plans. Life itself was such an exquisite privilege that the future was left to take care of itself. So while our American neighbors planned vacations and retirements, our parents' time and energy were consumed by the day-to-day chore of rebuilding a family in the tradition of the *alter heim*, the "Old Country." Holocaust survivors didn't worry about getting older, perhaps because they never had a chance to be young.

For my generation, the pursuit to "find" ourselves was not something we had witnessed in our parents. Yet paradoxically, it was they who gave us the capacity to engage in it. Their seriousness about survival, about devotion to family and community, their rock-solid commitment to our Torah-observant ways and *mesorah* – all this gave us a foundation upon which to build, to enhance our lives with dimensions and nuances that, to them, had been unattainable luxuries.

This spirit of living with affirmation and gusto – personified by my dear parents – accompanies us on this journey as well.

NOW THAT YOU KNOW a bit about me, you can understand why – when I reached my sixtieth birthday – I felt a strong sense of gratitude to the Almighty for bringing me to that milestone.

Today I have much for which to be thankful: I am healthy in mind and body and I now have the time and flexibility to engage in pursuits beyond my business endeavors. Miriam, my wife of four decades, is still my best friend and trusted partner. Together, we proudly watch our children and grandchildren grow up sharing our convictions and values. I am fortunate to have many relatives and friends whom I value, respect, and love. All of these blessings have given me the support and galvanized my spirit to write the volume you now hold in your hand.

This book is my foray into the world of kosher fine wine – an entity that came into existence during the past two decades. Possibly the best-kept secret in the world is that there are outstanding, subtle, complex kosher wines that have proven in international wine competition to be on par with, and even superior to, today's non-kosher wines. This fact will come as a surprise to the non-kosher wine aficionado, while it presents quandaries for the kosher consumer inexperienced in tasting fine wine. How should this new level of enjoyment be approached? What is the best way to develop appreciation for the remarkable wines available to us today? My hope is that I will enlighten you somewhat on this subject and give you the tools you need to embark on your own journey of discovery.

Irving Langer
Lawrence, New York
5772/2012

A Note to Readers

I occasionally use Hebrew and Yiddish terms because they are part of my life and that of most kosher wine consumers. If you are unfamiliar with these words, I urge you to make use of the glossary at the end of this book. There is also a glossary of wine terms because that, too, is a language in itself!

Acknowledgments

NO ONE WALKS ALONE, and when walking the journey of life, just where do you start to thank all those who walked beside you and helped along the way?

First, I would like to dedicate this book to my dear friend Danny Goldstein. His encouragement, enthusiasm, and love of fine wine inspired me to write this book. He made a number of useful suggestions that helped me clarify my thoughts. I find it difficult to express my indebtedness adequately. Thank you.

I am deeply grateful to my research team in Israel for the marvelous job they did. In particular, Nathan Gluck, a brilliant and learned rabbi, spent countless hours supplying me with the valuable information I needed.

Equally important is Ofer Zemach, a renowned photographer and connoisseur of fine wine. Thank you for taking me to the Israeli wineries and for your beautiful pictures.

Additional thanks to Benny Goldstein for his enthusiasm and endless energy. Your assistance to me was invaluable.

Rabbi Dovid Cohen, my Rebbe for the past twenty years, found time from his busy schedule to read parts of the manuscript and encourage publication.

Rabbi Shimon Susholz gave me my first taste of dry red wine every Shabbos during our weekly learning *shiur*. He, too, read and added balance to the book with his valuable knowledge.

Charlotte Friedland, a first-class editor, has a rare gift for lucid and succinct phraseology in a league of its own. I look forward to working with her again.

Rabbi Nahum Spirn edited chapter nine, "What Did the Sages Drink?" He meticulously verified the accuracy of this interesting chapter and brought my attention to sources I would not otherwise have encountered.

My wine-loving friends Aaron Munk, Josh Schupack, Meir Halpern, and Noach

Feingold reviewed the manuscript and gave me their much-needed professional advice.

My friends Rita Auerbach, Toby Klein, Naftali Manella, Fred and Esther Moskovitz gave constructive criticism and told me they hear me talking in the book.

My thanks to Sheila Selig for her help in coordinating the entire project beyond the call of duty – you are the best.

I would also like to express my appreciation to the staff at Gefen Publishing House, in particular Senior Editor Kezia Raffel Pride, whose talents and finesse took the manuscript and polished it until it shined.

Last – but certainly foremost – I thank my wife, Miriam, for her unlimited patience, numerous reviews, and spot-on corrections. You are my true *aishes chayil*, the strength of everything I do. May we continue to grow together and see much *Yiddishe nachas* from our children.

I was saddened to hear of the untimely passing of Daniel Rogov, *z"l*, whose zest for life and remarkable sensitivity to the subtle nuances of wine and food made him an icon in the industry. Certainly, his insight will be missed and impossible to replicate. Yet his legacy must and will continue.

Introduction

BY DANIEL ROGOV, Z"L

J ews probably have the oldest codified relationship of any people to wine. The Bible mentions wine hundreds of times, and it is evident that wine was not only an important element in every religious ritual but also an important staple in everyday life.

HISTORIANS ESTIMATE THAT THE ISRAELITES of the Second Temple period consumed about three hundred gallons annually and produced enormous quantities of wine not only for local consumption but also for export. Grape growing and wine making were important agriculture branches in the Israelite economy and there is plenty of evidence to this fact in the remains of hundreds of winepresses scattered throughout the Land of Israel. During the Roman period, Israeli wines were so highly prized that they were shipped not only to nobles in Rome, but also to Roman outposts throughout Europe and North Africa. Wine making in the Holy Land flourished from biblical times through the Byzantine era and came to an end only with the Islamic conquest of the country in the seventh century CE.

After the destruction of the Second Temple

(in approximately 70 CE), Jews continued to exercise their expertise in viticulture outside of the Land of Israel throughout the Roman Empire. They grew grapes, made wine, and traded in wines in many communities scattered through the countries of the Mediterranean. Family members of the great eleventh-century commentator Rashi were vintners, and Jews were also known as able vintners in Alsace, Spain, and Italy. Unfortunately, later in the Middle Ages, Jews were prohibited from owning land, and that put an end to their involvement in viticulture. From then on, they produced only small amounts of kosher wine for sacramental purposes, to be used mainly at home and made from table grapes or even from raisins and berries.

Jews who settled in North America continued to produce wines for sacramental purposes and only in the late nineteenth century did commercial production of kosher wines begin, mostly in New York State by firms like Manischewitz and Schapiro. Unfortunately, the wines were made from

Concord grapes and were coarse and bitter; they had to be sweetened in order to make them palatable. Over time, it was such sweet, unsophisticated wines that came to be associated with kosher wine. In the late 1950s, the Herzog family, owner of the Royal Wine Company, started to modernize the kosher wine industry and today they are producing kosher wines that are among the best in the world.

Along with Herzog, there are other fine producers of US kosher wines, among them Hagafen, Covenant, and Four Gates. The producers of first-grade kosher wines use noble grapes such as Cabernet Sauvignon, Syrah, Pinot Noir, and Chardonnay, and the very best producers of kosher wines in the United States are located today in California, where they benefit from the highly valued vineyards of the Napa and Sonoma Valleys and the Santa Cruz Mountains.

In Europe, the production of kosher wines beyond a cottage-industry level started in the 1980s with two large wineries, first Fortant de France in Provence and then Capçanes in Spain, who started to produce a line of kosher wines. Following the pattern set by Israel and California, these wineries relied on noble grapes and thoroughly modern production methods. Today, nearly every wine-growing region in Europe produces and exports kosher wines.

At the end of the nineteenth century, wine making was revived in the Holy Land. That happened largely due to the efforts of Baron Edmond de Rothschild, the owner of the famed Chateau Lafite in Bordeaux, who took the new Jewish colonies under his patronage. Rothschild funded the planting of numerous vineyards and built two large wineries, one in Rishon LeZion in 1882, and another in Zichron Ya'akov in 1890. In 1906 he helped set up a cooperative of grape growers that would manage the wineries, and this cooperative evolved to become Carmel Winery, one of the oldest and largest in Israel. Rothschild's dream that viticulture would provide a major source of income for the Jewish settlers was shattered with the advent of three  major events: the Russian Revolution, the enactment of Prohibition in the United States, and the banning of imported wines to Egypt. These factors virtually eliminated the fledgling industry's three largest potential markets.

The real revolution in Israeli wine started in 1972 when Professor Cornelius Ough of the Department of Viticulture and Enology at the University of California at Davis visited Israel and suggested that the soil and climate of the Golan Heights would prove ideal for raising grapes. In 1976, the first vines were planted in the Golan. It was soon apparent that Israel was capable of producing wines of world-class quality.

WHAT MAKES A WINE KOSHER?

WINES THAT ARE CERTIFIED kosher by rabbinic authorities adhere strictly to three fairly simple requirements:

• From the onset of the harvest, only kosher tools and storage facilities may be used in the wine-making process, and all of the wine-making equipment must be cleaned to be certain that no foreign objects remain in the equipment or vats.

• All the materials (e.g., yeasts) used in the production and clarification of the wines must be certified as kosher.

• From the moment the grapes reach the winery, only Sabbath-observant Jews come into contact with them.

Not many realize that there are differences between the requirements for a wine to be kosher within Israel and outside Israel. In order for an Israeli wine to be certified as kosher, it must meet the above requirements, and must also adhere to Jewish laws governing produce in the Holy Land. None of these requirements has a negative impact on the quality of the kosher wine, and several are widely acknowledged to be sound agricultural practices even by producers of non-kosher wines.

Wines labeled *mevushal* have the advantage that they can be opened and poured by non-Jews, which is particularly important at large public events, such as weddings. The Hebrew word *mevushal* simply means "cooked,"

indicating that the wine has been heated. In olden times, it was actually boiled, but that is not the case anymore. Today, after the grapes are crushed, the common practice is to rapidly raise the temperature of the liquids to 176–194°F in special flash pasteurizing units, hold it there for under a minute, and then return the temperature, equally rapidly, to 60°F. Modern technology has reduced the impact of these processes on the quality of the wine (though most winemakers feel that pasteurized wines do lose many of their essential essences, and may impart a "cooked" sensation to the nose and palate). Many *mevushal* wines will drink nicely for six months to a year after bottling, but nearly all will show signs of deterioration after that. A few producers, most notably those of the California wineries Hagafen and Herzog, have produced *mevushal* wines that are the equivalent in quality and perhaps even aging potential to their non-*mevushal* counterparts.

One word of friendly warning: all wineries in Israel and in the United States that produce kosher wines generally produce only kosher wines, but in France, Italy, Spain, and other European countries, as well as in South America, many wineries produce both kosher and non-kosher editions of the same wine. Consumers must check each bottle to see that appropriate kosher certification is present.

THE CHANGE IN JEWISH WINE DRINKING

WINE CONSUMPTION in the United States and Canada among those who observe the Jewish laws of *kashrus* now parallels that of the average American – a consumption of some nine to eleven liters of wine annually. This is considered moderate consumption by nearly all studies in the fields of medicine and epidemiology. Consumption of kosher wines in the United Kingdom among those who keep kosher is just a tad higher, some ten to eleven liters annually. Although there is some debate about precisely how much wine is being consumed by Israelis currently, recent years have seen a major increase, and consumption now stands at seven to eight liters annually.

The increase in consumption both in and outside of Israel reflects the increasing quality of kosher wines. It also reflects the fact that many more people are traveling abroad and dining in fine restaurants, where wine is an integral part of the meal. They have become accustomed to wine with their meals. Today, many are also touring the fine wineries of the Bordeaux, Tuscany, Napa, and Sonoma Valleys, and the five wine regions of Israel, particularly those of the Golan Heights. (See the chapter "Jewish Geography" for fascinating details on this.)

Not too long ago, I dined at the Tierra Sur restaurant in the Herzog Wine Cellars in Oxnard, California. I enjoyed such appetizers as chorizo lamb sausages with black olive piadina flatbread, a venison galantine with crispy lamb lardons, and a Jerusalem artichoke soup with a dab of toasted walnut oil for appetizers, followed by aged rib-eye steak with a red wine sauce, and a duet of duck composed of a confit of duck leg and seared duck breast with caramelized cippolini onions for entrées. Two fine wines were served with the meal: Goose Bay 2007 Pinot Gris from New Zealand, and Herzog's Special Reserve Zinfandel Lodi 2005. It was clear from the high quality of every dish that this was a truly fine restaurant, and it was all strictly kosher. In short,

contemporary kosher consumers need not settle for less than the finest wine and cuisine, and the data bears this out.

Equally worthy of attention is that in addition to showing a growing appreciation of wine in general, those who consume kosher wines are moving in several directions that can also be seen among the general population. Wine consumption is shifting from semi-dry to dry wines, from whites to reds, from light to heavier wines and, most importantly, there is a movement toward buying higher-quality wines. Twenty-five years ago, more than 90 percent of the kosher wines produced in the world were sweet. Today, over 80 percent of the kosher wines produced are dry, and the best of those that are made sweet are done so at great expense in order to produce some of the very best dessert wines.

GRAPE VARIETIES USED FOR KOSHER WINES

IN THE CHAPTER TITLED "Charting Our Course," you will learn of six of the many varieties of "noble" grapes: Riesling, Chardonnay, Sauvignon, Pinot Noir, Merlot,  and Cabernet Sauvignon. I would like to add to these the following grape varieties most likely to be encountered in kosher wines. After you familiarize yourself with the basics, you will be able to refer back to this list with greater understanding. While I am trying to avoid excessive jargon, in my descriptions I may use the term *tannins*: these are natural components in the grape that give wines their relative "dry" qualities.

Red Wine Grapes

Barbera. From Italy's Piedmont region, this grape has the potential for producing wines that, although light and fruity, are capable of great charm.

Cabernet Franc. Less intense and softer than Cabernet Sauvignon, most often destined to be blended with Merlot and Cabernet Sauvignon, but even on its own capable of producing dramatically good, leafy, fruity, and aromatic reds.

Carignan. An old-timer on the kosher scene, for many years this originally Spanish grape produced largely dull wines. In recent years, however, several wineries have demonstrated that old-vine Carignan grapes, especially those from fields that were not irrigated for many years, can produce interesting and high-quality wines.

Gamay. The well-known grape of France's Beaujolais region, this fairly recent introduction to the kosher wine scene is capable of producing light- to medium-bodied wines of fragrance and charm, intended primarily for drinking in their youth.

Grenache. Although this grape has traditionally done well in France's Rhone Valley and Spain, for many years it did not yield sophisticated kosher wines, most being somewhat pale, overripe, and sweet in nature. Today, however, there is a growing move to cut back on the yield of the grape, the result being sometimes concentrated and intense wines of long cellaring potential.

Malbec. Well known in France's Bordeaux, the Loire, and Cahors, and the specialty grape of Argentina, this grape is capable of producing dense, rich, tannic, spicy wines that are remarkably dark in color.

Nebbiolo. The grape from which the Barolo and Barbaresco wines of Italy's Piedmont region are made. Still experimental in Israel and California, but with the potential for producing perfumed, fruity, and intense wines with full body and high tannins, acidity, and color, this grape produces wines capable of long-term cellaring.

Petit Verdot. Planted only in small quantities and used in Bordeaux primarily for blending with other noble varieties to add acidity and balance, this grape on its own yields long-lived and tannic wine.

Petite Sirah. Even though related only peripherally to the great Syrah grape, this grape is, at its best, capable of producing dark, tannic, and well-balanced wines of great appeal and sophistication. For many years it was used to produce mass-market wines that tended to be hot, tannic, and without charm. The potential of this grape is now being well demonstrated both in California and in Israel in an increasing number of truly excellent wines.

Pinotage. A South African cross between Pinot Noir and Cinsault, capable of being flavorful and powerful yet soft and full, with a pleasing sweet finish and a lightly spicy overlay.

Sangiovese. Italy's most frequently planted variety, found in the simplest Chianti and most complex Brunello di Montalcino wines. Recently introduced to the kosher world, it is showing fine results, with wines that are lively, fruity, and full of charm.

Syrah. Some believe that this grape originated in ancient Persia and was brought to France by the Romans, while others speculate that it is indigenous to France. Syrah found its first glory in France's northern Rhone Valley, and then in Australia, where it is known as Shiraz. Capable of producing deep royal purple

tannic wines that are full-bodied enough to be thought of as dense and powerful, but with excellent balance and complex aromas and flavors of plums, berries, currants, black pepper, and chocolate. First kosher results from this grape have been exciting.

Tempranillo. The staple grape of Spain's Rioja area, with recent plantings in Israel, it has the potential for producing long-lived complex and sophisticated wines typified by aromas and flavors of black fruits, leather, tobacco, and spices.

Zinfandel. Although Zinfandel, the Italian variety of which is known as Primitivo, is an old staple in California, it is relatively new in Israel. Until recently the kosher wines produced were largely charmless semi-dry blush wines, those often referred to as "White Zin." Recently planted high-quality vines from California and in Israel offer the potential for producing full-bodied to massive wines, moderately to highly alcoholic, with generous tannins and the kind of warm berry flavors that typify these wines at their best.

White Wine Grapes

Chenin Blanc. Originating in France's central Loire Valley, a grape capable of producing long-lived wines with honeyed notes. Until recently used in Israel to produce ordinary, semi-dry wines, but now being shown by several small wineries to produce exciting dry and sweet wines.

Gewürztraminer. This grape originated in Germany, came to its glory in Alsace, and has now been transplanted to many parts of the world. It is capable of producing aromatic

dry and sweet wines that are often typified by their softness and spiciness, as well as by distinctive aromas and flavors of lychees and rose petals.

Muscat. There are many varieties of Muscat, the three most often used being Muscat of Alexandria, Muscat Canelli, and Black Muscat, each of which is capable of producing wines that range from the dry to the sweet. Muscats are almost always typified by their perfumed aromas.

Emerald Riesling. This is a cross between the Muscadelle and Riesling grapes developed in California primarily for growth in warm climates; it produces mostly semi-dry wines.

Semillon. Although this native French grape was used for many years in Israel and South Africa to produce largely low-quality semi-dry white wines, its susceptibility to noble rot is now being used to advantage to produce sweet dessert wines with the distinctive bouquet and flavors of melon, fig, and citrus. Several small wineries have recently begun producing interesting dry whites from this grape.

Traminette. A not overly exciting hybrid, a derivative of the Gewürztraminer grape, developed primarily for use in cold-weather New York State and Canadian climates.

Viognier. This grape produces the fascinating Condrieu wines of France's Rhone Valley. It yields aromatic but crisply dry whites and full-bodied whites, some of which have long aging potential.

HOW CAN WE DECIDE WHICH WINES ARE BEST FOR US?

THE BEST WINES are those that give you the most satisfaction. The question that remains for many is precisely how to identify those wines.

The best way is to taste wines. After you read this book, you will know how to do this, and you will discover the wonderful new adventure of wine tasting.

The more we taste, the easier it is to make our selections. You may find wine-tasting events at your local wine shops that carry kosher wines. Another good bet is to attend the various kosher wine or wine/food fairs and festivals that are held in many places within the United States.

Even tasting may not be enough, however, for it is difficult to keep up with the more than fifteen hundred kosher wines that are now released every year. The major way to keep track of all the new wines is to follow one or more wine critics whose integrity and palates you trust. It also pays to develop a work- ing relation- ship with the staff of the wine shops at which you purchase wine

most often. Their recommendations can be relied upon as they come to know your tastes.

A FEW WORDS ABOUT WINE LANGUAGE

SOME PEOPLE consider wine language intimidating. They are deterred by terms such as body, acidity, balance, tannins, oak-aging, drinking windows, and taste and scent associations such as blackberries, black currants, smoky oak, chocolate, espresso coffee, and roasted herbs. However, if you think of the terminology of art, mathematics, or music, you will realize that wine language makes sense.

True, some of the people who toss those terms around are nothing more than wine snobs, showing off. On the other hand, truly knowledgeable people, be they winemakers, wine critics, or consumers, use these terms in order to best describe their experience in tasting wine. Without at least a basic knowledge of any field, one cannot discuss or fully understand it. You will find definitions of crucial terms as you go along in this book, and there is also a glossary of terms that will help you decode the language of wine. Your new vocabulary undoubtedly will lead you to a fuller, finer appreciation of the quality kosher wines available today.

I'm sure you will find Irving Langer's book informative and enjoyable.

Part 1

UNDERSTANDING WINE

CHAPTER ONE

Before You Enter the World of Kosher Fine Wine

Here is your first step toward understanding and appreciating fine wine: *Free your mind!*

All the rest is commentary.

But the commentary is necessary and worthwhile. Before we revel in our unprecedented opportunities to enjoy fine wine, we need to stop and think about wine from a Jewish perspective.

MOST OF US are children or grandchildren of people who struggled just to survive in the Old Country. Our ancestors could not be certain about anything in life. I think that deep down inside, many Jews suffer from a certain discomfort about how good we have it. We are hindered by a survivor mentality that focuses on fulfilling needs instead of experiencing pleasure, and this interferes with our ability to appreciate the finer things that G-d put into this world for our enjoyment.

As I look back on my younger years, I know that I was imbued with this attitude by my family and community. If you have decent food to eat and a dry place to sleep, be grateful! I know that's true on one level – we are "entitled" to nothing, and everything we have from Heaven is a gift. But I truly feel that we need to move on, to accept those gifts graciously, unwrap them, and put them to use in ways that will make us better people.

Some of us may yearn to go back to a simpler time, but let's be honest: we can't go back. And we would be foolish and ungrateful if we tried. If G-d put us in this era of plenty, we should appreciate this goodness without feeling guilty about it.

About 350 years ago, many Torah sages had already begun to feel that a change was coming over human beings, at least in our culture. Prior to that time, it was understood that any seriously spiritual person must attempt to break and subdue the flesh through mortifications and fasts. However, the Ba'al Shem Tov, the father of the Chassidic movement, pointed out that people were becoming physically weaker and more prone to feelings of depression, hopelessness, and low self-esteem. He taught that we need to do whatever we can to maintain a positive, optimistic, and joyous

> ## Jewish Jokes Reveal a Lifestyle
>
> A typical joke from prewar Europe underscores how common privation was back in the day. It is about Herschel of Ostropol, a legendary prankster and the enduring symbol of Jewish resourcefulness in the face of adversity. One day, Herschel walked into an inn and asked for food. The innkeeper asked him if he had any money. Herschel replied, "You had better feed me or else I will have to do what my father used to do!"
>
> "I would prefer that you pay," said the owner.
>
> "If you don't feed me," cried Herschel in a loud voice, "I will do what my father and my grandfather would do!"
>
> Somewhat taken aback, the owner replied a little sheepishly, "You know, people usually pay in restaurants…"
>
> "IF YOU DON'T FEED ME," yelled Herschel in a crazy, booming voice, "I WILL DO WHAT MY FATHER, MY GRANDFATHER, AND MY GREAT-GRANDFATHER WOULD DO!"
>
> Not wanting a scene, the innkeeper relented and gave Herschel a bowl of soup. When Herschel finished eating, the innkeeper asked, "Tell me – what would your father, grandfather, and great-grandfather do if they didn't get food?"
>
> "Oh, that's simple," replied Hershel. "They would go to bed hungry."

state of mind, conducive to serving G-d. Enjoying fine wine with an enlightened state of mind focused on appreciating His bounty does precisely this. As it says in Psalms (104:15), "Wine gladdens the human heart!"

WALKING A FINE LINE

BEFORE YOU CONCLUDE that I'm advocating all-out hedonism, let's get back to Jewish basics. The truth is that many of us eat without thinking; the mind is focused on something else while we allow the body to fill its needs. Guess what! Thoughtless eating is almost always excessive eating. We eat and drink in a haze of inattention and wonder why we eat too much. But wise people understand that in order to eat and drink within reasonable limits we have to be aware; we have to enjoy our food! The purpose of drinking wine with our meals is to open the palate to better enjoy the food. Bringing the mind and body together in a pleasurable experience does not make us gluttons; it makes us more balanced and healthier.

Instead of pursuing just bodily satisfaction, we should experience the pleasure of appreciating the beauty and wonder of creation, the wonder of a beautiful day, the brilliance of a great piece of music, and yes, the joy of our senses as we discover the complex tastes and aromas of a really fine wine.

Having pleasure is not an obsession with physicality. It means refining your personality and your palate to appreciate subtlety. It means becoming an individual with an open mind and a depth of feeling. These are additional dimensions of life and they are uplifting, even if they are connected to physical experiences. They begin as physical, but they take you beyond the physical.

A perfect example of this principle is Shabbos food. No one can deny that we go to great lengths to prepare delicacies for Shabbos, and our tables are laden with the highest-quality cuisine we can afford. Yet the essence of Shabbos is entirely spiritual.

Is there a contradiction between the transcendent concept of Shabbos and our feasts?

No. Judaism is focused on utilizing everything material to approach the spiritual. That is why we say a blessing on our food before and after we eat; we are aligning ourselves with spirituality even as we feed our bodies. It is a *mitzvah* to reserve the finest foods for Shabbos because when we eat properly (without excess and with full awareness), the food elevates our Shabbos experience. Pious people stop and look at everything they eat and say, "In honor of the holy Shabbos" before taking a bite.

Arza Winery, 1970s ▲

SO WHAT DOES THE TORAH SAY?

BY NOW, my contention should be clear to you: sensitizing and refining yourself to appreciate subtle realities is very much in line with Torah values. When I enjoy a great glass of wine, it brings me closer to the uplifting wonder I find in a Talmudic discussion or an insightful Midrash. The Gemara (*Bava Basra* 12b) hints at this effect: "One who routinely drinks wine – even if his heart is totally stopped up – the wine will make him intelligent!" My experience is that good wine opens the heart and the mind.

I am convinced that the fine kosher wines being produced today provide us with an opportunity to relearn the skill that the sages of the Talmud certainly possessed: the ability to experience pleasure as uplifting and edifying.

There is a well-known question in the Gemara (*Nedarim* 10b) about a *nazir* (one who has sworn off drinking wine for a specific period of time in order to rectify a personal failing or to rise to a higher spiritual level through abstinence). The Talmud asks: if he has reached a special level of sanctity, why is he required to bring a sin offering to the Holy Temple? The response is that the *nazir* has "sinned against his soul" by refusing himself wine. This Gemara is taken rightly as an indication that one should not abstain from legitimate pleasure.

It's interesting to note that wine parallels spirituality in that it improves with age. As a rule, physical things get weaker and deteriorate with age. Wine is one of the few exceptions![1]

There is another fascinating revelation in the Gemara (*Sanhedrin* 98a) that when *Eretz Yisrael* – our Holy Land of Israel – begins to produce fruit for us, it is a clear sign that Redemption is on its way. To me it is obvious that the production of fine kosher wine in Israel is part of this wonderful sign, one we should recognize and cherish.

Our ancestors had a very well-developed wine culture that was both pleasurable and spiritual. During our long exile, we lost this heritage, but it is now being restored to us little by little. I hope that this book will open new vistas for you, so that you too will be able to reclaim a healthy Jewish respect and appreciation of this unique, spiritually charged drink.

---

[1] Thank you to Rabbi Nahum Spirn for this insight.

CHAPTER TWO
Roll Out the Barrel!

A famous Midrash recounts a remarkable conversation between the Roman general Turnus Rufus and Rabbi Akiva. The soldier asks the sage why Jews circumcise their newborn boys, adding cynically, "Do you think you can improve upon G-d's creation?" Rabbi Akiva retorts, "What's better – wheat kernels or bread?" The general answers, "The latter, of course."

"So too," says the sage, "our job is to be G-d's partners by perfecting His creations" (*Midrash Tanchuma, Tazria #5*).

FOLLOWING THIS principle, making wine is a process of perfecting grapes. In fact, the outcome of this process creates an entirely new entity requiring us to say the unique Hebrew blessing over wine, *borei pri hagafen:* "[Blessed are You]...Who creates the fruit of the vine." This blessing does not apply to any other "fruit juice" or food. Moreover, even when the blessing of *hamotzi* is said over bread at the start of a meal, it covers all foods in the meal – except wine! We are bidden to bless the wine with its own special blessings before we drink it.

When you think about it, wine and bread have a lot in common. Both start as a raw product from the earth that is harvested by Man, who works on it, refines it, changes it, combines it with other ingredients, and creates a wonderful, new, nourishing substance. And because of this, they both have a certain spiritual quality and power not found in other foods or beverages.

Perhaps even more than bread, the making of fine wine is a science, an art, and a labor of love. Every step of the process will impact on the taste, aroma, and quality of the wine, and could spell the difference between an undrinkable concoction, a mediocre beverage, and a superlative fine wine. It's a wisdom that goes back as far as Noah, perhaps back to Creation, and it is still developing!

It takes expertise, intelligence, creativity, and enormous blessing from Above to make really good wine. To me, understanding the efforts that went into producing the liquid sparkling in my glass increases my respect and appreciation.

So let's look at what a grape goes through before it reaches your lips as a luscious drop of wine. We're talking here about table wine, the kind used most frequently, also known as natural or still wines (as opposed to bubbly types). Because the process is intricate and has variations, I can only give you the broad outlines. But believe me – even a glimpse will increase your reverence for this noble drink and those who labor to perfect it.

In the Beginning...

Wine is the fermented juice of grapes, and though roughly four thousand varieties of grapes have been developed from one species (*vitis vinifera*, if you're into Latin), only about a dozen are normally used in wine making. Grapes from this species contain natural sugar, and after fermentation (explained in this chapter), wine is produced with an alcohol content that varies roughly from 7 percent to more than 10 percent by volume.

As you know, grapes come in a variety of colors, ranging from green-yellow to red and blue-black. Yet the juice from almost all of them is colorless. Red wines and rosés derive their color from the grape skins during processing.

THE SCIENCE OF WINE MAKING

IN LATER CHAPTERS, we will discuss the *terroir* factor – a French term suggesting that the precise location of where a vine grows will affect its grapes.

For now, let's say the grapes have been planted and harvested. The basic steps of wine making are crushing, juice separation, treatment of the "must" (which is the mass of crushed grapes and juice), fermentation, racking, clarification, aging, and bottling. There are a great many variations to this process, but this is a thumbnail sketch.

Crushing

No peasants with bare feet participate in this stage anymore. Today, grapes are thrown into a crusher and/or de-stemmer, which takes the grapes off their stems and crushes the skins so the juice can flow.

Separation

A winepress gently pushes the grape pulp against a perforated drum. White wine grapes are pressed before fermentation, and grapes used for red wine are pressed afterward.

Fermentation

In large vats (that prevent oxidation), yeast (kosher yeast in kosher wine) is added to "eat" the sugars that are in the grapes, producing a

chemical reaction in which the sugar in the grape juice is turned into alcohol and carbon dioxide. This is what turns grape juice into wine. In red wine production, the juice, skins, and seeds are fermented together. Some white wines may be fermented in oak barrels to preserve their fruity flavor. Fermentation can take from ten to forty days, and temperature control is critical to promote yeast growth and to extract flavors and colors from skins (in red wine).

When red wine is fermenting, the pulp and skins tend to float to the top, which forms a cap. Because the cap can cause the temperature to rise in the vat and reduce the extraction of color and flavor, the cap must be submerged, as often as twice daily. In some large vats, the "must" is drawn off from the bottom of the vat and pumped back in over the cap. Some wines are fermented more than once.

Racking

Now there is a mixture of wine and sediment (of dead yeast cells, called lees) and they must be separated. The wine is racked – i.e., moved to new, clean barrels – so the suspended particles can settle. In some wines, the particles drop quickly to the bottom, but other wines can remain cloudy for quite a while.

Clarifying and Filtering

Various processes can be used to clarify the wine and remove the sediment. (Kosher wines do not use all of the commonly used processes or fining ingredients.) The wine may be filtered, though not necessarily. Most wines go through a very fine filter to clear all sediments. A number of vineyards are choosing not to do this, claiming the technique takes away certain deli-

cious flavors. The majority still do filter. Fining is another technique, done by adding a precipitating agent to a wine to remove or at least reduce the concentration of unwanted particles.

Aging

In a wooden barrel, oxygen can slowly enter the wine, and water and alcohol can escape. While resting in a barrel, wine goes

through subtle chemical changes, resulting in greater complexity and softening of the harsh tannins and flavors present at the end of fermentation. The character of the wood is also absorbed by the wine and additional clarification may happen. The wood-aging process can take a few months or several years. It's a delicate procedure,

though. Leaving the wine too long in barrels can destroy some of the grape flavor and result in wine that tastes too "woody."

Bottling

Some wines are aged for a long time, while others are not – but lack of aging doesn't imply that the wine is of low quality. Either way, after the wine is clarified through settling and/or filtering, it will be bottled. Small wineries may still bottle by hand, but most use enclosed, highly sterile apparatus to keep impurities from getting into the wine. After that, some wines will be left to age in the bottle; others will be sold right away. One of the reasons some wine bottles have a portion raised in the

center of the base is to allow settling along the edges, so the wine is clear when you pour it. If you see deposits around the bottom of the bottle, it does not mean that the wine is bad: it's more likely intentionally unfiltered, which is preferred by some winemakers. If there is stuff floating inside the wine, that's a different story.

Arza Winery, 1970s

Clarifying and Filtering photo courtesy of Ella Valley Winery

THE SCOOP ON BARRELS

NOW WHAT ABOUT THOSE barrels? Winemakers are finicky about what barrels they use, and some have barrels made especially for them. Cooperage (the art of making barrels) and wine making are so entwined that it's hard to talk about one without the other. In a world where goods are rarely shipped in barrels anymore, the wine industry keeps the cooper's art alive. While you might think that storing and aging wine in wooden containers is an outdated practice, even in the most modern wineries some wines are still fermented or matured in good old wood. Due to its strength and workability, oak is the universal wood of choice. Its relatively tight grain permits a more gradual extraction of wood flavors and minimizes wine loss through evaporation. It is flexible, enabling the staves (thin slats of wood making up the sides) to be bent without breaking.

The main purpose of aging wine in barrels, as mentioned above, is to fine-tune its taste by adding delicate flavors of oak. Winemakers, who have extremely sensitive palates, try to bring out a huge variety of flavors from the oak, flavors that are best described as spicy, toasty, buttery, and vanilla-like. (When your senses for wine are well developed, you will smell and taste these flavors too.)

When you consider how subtle every aspect of wine making is, you can understand why even the origin of the wood in the barrels makes a difference. French oak (of course!) and American oak are some of the world's best-known barrels for aging wine. The way the wood is handled, together with the preparation of the barrel during construction, also affects the quality and taste of the wine. So does the intensity of the "toasting" process the barrel has undergone: the inside of the barrel is heated, just so, during its construction to caramelize the flavors. There are slight differences between the two types of oak that are reflected in the flavor and characteristics they impart. French oak is thought to be more subtle, with vanilla characteristics, while the American oak is more powerful and toasty.

An embarrassing fact is that when American coopers began making oak wine barrels, the results were not good: the wine inside them just didn't achieve true quality. At first, it was speculated that the wood itself was deficient. But when French methods for preparing the wood and building the barrels were tried on American oak, the results were terrific. Now that French techniques are utilized in the United States, American oak barrels are in use all over the world. Score another one for the French.

Choosing the right barrel requires knowledge and experience. The smaller the barrel, the greater the proportion of the wine inside it that touches the barrel's surfaces, allowing the wine to extract more flavors. But there is much more to it than that. The type of barrel the winemaker will select is a matter of tradition, wine variety, economy, and of course, personal taste.

A barrel holds approximately sixty gallons of wine. The inner walls of the barrels are toasted before use; a high level of toasting produces a charcoal layer between the wood and the wine. When the character of the wine is strong we say it is "toasted."

CHAPTER THREE

Charting Our Course

I'm a great lover of maps. Back in the days before GPS, whenever I took a trip to a distant city, I would always invest in a good map. Far more important than just keeping me oriented, it spares me from having to ask every passerby for directions. I never get lost – though sometimes I'm unaware of our precise location. I guess women would call me a "typical man" because I see no point in pulling over to ask some clueless pedestrian or disinterested teenager the way to my destination. Who knows whether the pedestrian is even familiar with the territory? If you can get the teen to take the earbuds out of his ear, there's no guarantee that he knows how to get there either. So just give me a good map. I'll find my way.

WHEN I BEGAN TO TASTE wine seriously, I was wandering around without a map. I was thinking in terms of bottles and labels, randomly trying one after another, but I had no concept that wines fall into categories that can be easily charted, if you know how. And like a driver without a map, I was forced to ask friends for direction. I imagine that most beginners do the same thing.

One day, you'll decide to try a bottle of Shiraz 2004, and the next day you might pick one that says Syrah 2007 on the label. Funny, they taste sort of the same. That's because Syrah and Shiraz are the same kind of grape with different names. Don't worry. We all did that – taking shots in the dark, with no sense of direction.

Eventually, you will discover that wine tasting is a unique world, and when you get oriented to it, you will find yourself making much better choices and getting richer experiences from your wine-tasting sessions. And that's why I'm here to give you your first geography lesson. I would like to familiarize you with the six major grape varieties, and the best way to do that is to visualize a map with three islands.

MY MAP: THREE IMAGINARY ISLANDS AND SIX CHASSIDIC COURTS

WHEN I THINK OF assorted wines and the experiences that go with tasting them, I am reminded of different kinds of Chassidic groups. To outsiders, they may all look the same, but when you get to know them, you discover that each group of Chassidim has its own texture and feeling, often based

upon the personality of the Rebbe who founded the group. Some Chassidic groups are very outgoing. Some turn inward. Some dance and sing a lot. Some are very serious. Some especially prize learning, while others particularly emphasize the development of heartfelt devotion. And like all living beings, each group wants to expand into new territory, stretching the limits of their experience.

Let me explain what this analogy has to do with my wine map! Imagine that there are three islands. At the bottom right of the map is a big island called Dry. Adjacent to it, at the bottom left, is a second, smaller island called Sweet. North of the first two islands is a third, even smaller one, called Sparkling.

Now imagine that there are two basic groups of Chassidim: let's call one group the "White Chassidim," and the second group the "Red Chassidim." Both the Whites and the Reds originated on Dry Island. The original White Rebbe, who lived many years ago, was a lofty, intellectual type, with impeccable manners. He was calm, sweet tempered, noble, and clearheaded. He valued cleanliness and moderation.

The original Red Rebbe was quite a different personality. He was down-to-earth, friendly, and very emotional. He had great depth of feeling, and was even prone to joyous outbursts. He was physically strong and robust, and was always happy to help others.

Over time, the White Chassidim and the Red Chassidim grew and split up into smaller groups. Because they got along well, sometimes they'd intermarry, so that smaller "Pink," "Blush," or "Rosé" families developed.

On the whole, the White Chassidim are very fond of high places with lots of air, and light, crisp breezes, since this fits their clearheaded, intellectual *derech* (way of life). The Red Chassidim prefer shady forests with deep canyons, where they can pour out their hearts in prayer and celebration. Each group has three major subgroups – let's call them Chassidic Courts – and numerous smaller ones. Some Chassidic Courts took their names from the cities where they originated, although the names were slightly altered and Yiddishized. Others based their names on aspects of their favored habitat. Here are the six major Chassidic Courts:

1 The lightest and airiest of the White Chassidim are called *Rizlinger Chassidim.* They live at the highest snowy altitudes. They strive to be clear minded and fresh like a high mountain breeze. They are also very good-natured, so they can be sweet as well. They love the tangy fruits that grow at their altitude.

2 Lower down on the slopes, the *Chardonner Chassidim* make their home. They focus on being well balanced and friendly to everyone. They are also blessed with liveliness and vitality. Like the Rizlinger Chassidim, they also enjoy the fresh tastes of plentifully grown fruit.

4 The highest-dwelling court of the Red Chassidim is that of the *Shishkener Chassidim.* *Shishke* means "pine cone" in Yiddish, and this court gets its name from the pine trees that grow in the upper forests. You would think they would be a rough, prickly bunch, but in actuality, they are softhearted, passionate, and caring. They love weddings and other emotional events and their singing easily brings people to tears.

3 Lower still on the mountain slopes, at the edge of the forest, are the *Vildeh Vaiseh Chassidim.* Their name means "Wild White." You see, even though they are lofty "White Chassidim," they can still be unpredictable, sharp, and a little aggressive. So they are considered a little wild in temperament. They appreciate spontaneity.

6 The last of the major Red Chassidic Courts makes its home in the deep shady canyons below the mountains. They call themselves the *Cabsover Chassidim*. Oddly, they don't really know how they got that name. In any event, they are large, hearty, and robust people. Whatever they do, they do with gusto. When they sing, they can be heard all the way up the mountain; when they dance, the ground shakes. But perhaps the most amazing thing about a Cabsover Chassid is that he can relate to anyone in any predicament and provide good advice in all situations! His soul can carry so much information and wisdom – it is quite amazing!

5 Lower down, the thick forests at the base of the mountains are home to the *Shvartz-Fogel Chassidim*. They are named after the blackbirds of the forest. Like other Red Chassidim, they have strong character, but they also value peace and tranquillity. A Shvartz-Fogel Chassid, with his friendly good nature, can settle any dispute and make everyone happy.

One day, the White Chassidim and the Red Chassidim set forth from Dry Island to colonize Sweet Island, hoping to establish many new communities. Sweet Island has mostly high altitudes, so the Reds didn't get a very good foothold. Nevertheless, some of the Reds did figure out how to survive. The Pink/Rosé families did somewhat better. As you can imagine, the Whites loved it, and eventually the Sweet Whites achieved many extraordinary things, becoming the stuff of legends.

In the next stage of their history, the White and Red Chassidim from both islands set off to explore the third island, Sparkling. At first, the Whites had the advantage, although lately more Reds have been making their home on Sparkling Island. Fortunately, there is plenty of room and resources for everybody, so all the Chassidic courts get along well, celebrating their diversity: the Dry Reds, the Dry Whites, the Sweet Reds, and the Sweet Whites. While many pride themselves on their pure heritage, one look at their extended family trees will reveal the wonderful blends that have resulted from their cordial intermarriages.

MEET THE BIG SIX

I'M SURE YOU GET MY DRIFT. The Red and White Chassidim represent the two major classifications of grapes, the reds and the whites. Needless to say, the islands represent the kinds of wines that the grape varieties can produce. Each grape variety is divided into smaller subdivisions. It is common to speak of "the Big Six" varieties, which are the most commonly cultivated. Of course, there are many other significant varieties. But if you know the Big Six, you have a solid base of knowledge to which you can add as you experience wines made from other grape varieties.

I placed the White Chassidim higher up on the mountain than Red Chassidim, simply to convey something about the character of the wines. The whites will give you more of a light, crisp, and airy feeling, while the reds will impart a deep, earthy, or woody taste.

Wines can be categorized and arranged from "lightest" to "deepest." The deeper the wine, the more powerful is its kick as it goes down. Deeper wines can also have more complexity, since they have the strength of character

needed to hold everything together. (More about "complexity" later.) In general, a light wine (whether red or white) will have more fruity tastes and aromas as well as more hints of sweetness. Often they will exhibit a kind of peachy taste, which needs (in my opinion) to be balanced by the wine's tartness and clarity so as not to render a queasy, unpleasant sensation.

So, now we're ready to learn the Big Six varieties. As you will see, their names are either German or French. They don't necessarily mean much in themselves, and in some cases nobody really knows their origin. I will provide you with some commonly believed hypotheses.

In the list that follows, the first three are white wines and the second three red, in order from lightest to deepest:

1 RIESLING [pronounced *Reezling*]. This German variety goes back to the Rhine region of Germany during the fifteenth century, when it was called Reusseling. The name is something of a mystery, but could have derived from characteristics of the vine itself. *Russ* is a dark wood, and *rissig* refers to grooved bark. Some speculate that the term *riessen* (to tear, or pull apart) may be part of the name. The grape is naturally acidic and tart and it can exhibit a wide variety of fruity flavors and aromas. Riesling grapes are strongly influenced by their location, so you can hardly know what a Riesling wine will be like unless you know where its vineyard was located. It ages well, and when it gets really old, it can exhibit a rubbery smell. This is actually considered a desirable quality in the wine because it adds something interesting to its character. Many sweet white wines are made from this grape.

2 CHARDONNAY [*Shar-doh-nay*]. Named after a village in Burgundy, France, this is a strong, energetic vine that grows well all over the world. The Chardonnay grape is somewhat neutral in taste. It is also easily influenced by its location and how it is fermented and aged. An aged Chardonnay can develop a buttery kind of texture. It is also used extensively for making Champagne and other sparkling wines. Chardonnay coming from cool climates can exhibit many flavors, from nuts and berries to tropical fruit tastes, while warm-climate Chardonnay can develop honey and vanilla flavors.

3 SAUVIGNON BLANC [*Soh-vee-nyohn Blahn*].[1] Its name means "wild white," which seems to indicate that the Sauvignon Blanc grape once grew wild. It is indigenous to the Bordeaux region of France. The wine produced from this grape

---

[1] Both these words end with a nasal sound that is difficult to represent in English. You can either say the English *n*, or, if you want to sound more authentic, the French nasal sound is like the sound you would make if you started saying the *ng* at the end of a word in English (for example, *song*) and stopped just before saying the *g* sound. It is a soft *n* sound, not fully pronounced, preceded by a nasal vowel sound such as that produced when you plug your nose!

Pinot Noir grapes ▶

is often said to have a grassy, herbal, and aggressive aroma, although it can also be crisp and refreshing. This grape is also often used in sparkling wines.

4 PINOT NOIR [*Pee-noh Nwahr*]. The name means "black pinecone" and it probably refers to the way the dark grapes cling together in closely packed clusters. The name may also derive from the noble family named Pinot that thrived during the Roman era, as this grape was being cultivated in the Burgundy region of France (Gaul) when the Romans invaded it in the first century. Wine made from these grapes is said to have sensual, intoxicating, sweet, and fruity tastes or aromas. The wine can exhibit a wide array of qualities that are often difficult to pin down. Some say that this is the most "romantic" of wines. It is light and soft.

5 MERLOT [*Mehr-loh*]. The name means "young blackbird," which may refer to the color of the grape. Or perhaps it means that blackbirds are fond of eating them. No one really knows. Merlot is thought of as being soft and friendly, with tastes of cherries or berries. Traditionally, it has been used to blend with stronger wines to balance out their sharper qualities. Nowadays, many pure Merlots are enjoyed as well. For the most part, such wines are considered easy-going, relaxed, and well-rounded, like an old friendship. Beginners should be aware that the Italian Merlots are lighter and easier to appreciate than their French or Californian cousins. Israeli Merlots also go down easy; softer and more supple, they are able to produce an opulent taste in the plummy category.

6 CABERNET SAUVIGNON [*Cab-ehr-nay Soh-vee-nyohn*]. Sometimes called Cab or Cab-so for short, this is a hybrid resulting from a chance crossing of Cabernet Franc and Sauvignon Blanc, probably in the seventeenth century. As mentioned above, Sauvignon Blanc is a "wild white" grape variety. The word *franc* just means "pure." The word *Cabernet* is a bit esoteric, though, and one theory is that it means "coal black," because the grape is very dark. It became popular in the 1800s, some calling it the king of red grapes, because it is a hardy plant and easier to grow than many other grape varieties.

Never a wimpy wine, Cab is known for its Big Taste. It can contain layers upon layers of tastes, aromas, and textures. It has such strong tannins that some Cabs are just undrinkable until they have aged, preferably in oak barrels. (Tannins are the organic substances from the seeds, stems, and grape skins that give wine its velvety, or drying, texture on the palate.) Even when aged, a Cab can still be too strong for beginners to enjoy. Once you get used to it, you will learn to appreciate its richness, its earthy flavors, and its woody undertones, as well as the spicy, tobacco, berry, or vanilla flavors that come popping up. It can also exhibit a wide variety of fruity tastes. A great Cab can be a like a symphony of sensations that hits you with force and assertiveness.

The first wine of the Big Six, Riesling, is super crisp, airy, and clear, while the sixth, Cabernet Sauvignon, is exceptionally strong, earthy, and robust. All the rest fall out somewhere in between. There are many other grape varieties, of course, but these are the basic ones.

You may be wondering why I didn't mention semi-dry or semi-sweet as wine categories. In truth, there are so many in-between varieties that adding more islands would clutter our map, and then we'd get lost trying to navigate around them. And the fact is that a wine's sweetness is not determined by the variety of grape itself, but the amount of sugar it contains. If it has a good amount of sugar, it is sweet. If it has no sugar whatsoever, it's as dry as last year's Pesach matzo. If it has a relatively small amount of sugar, it's called semi-sweet or semi-dry. Personally, I believe you can draw the line where you like, but to me a wine is basically either dry or sweet.

How Can Something Wet Be Dry?

Dry simply means that all the natural sugar in the grapes was fermented into alcohol and there is no residual sugar (RS) left. How the term dry came to mean "not sweet" is a bit of a mystery. Even wine experts seem indecisive about its origin, but "dry" seems to go back to the Middle Ages when the French term vin sec (dry wine) was used in a play. We have no idea whether the term was already in common use or the playwright invented it, perhaps as a witty description of the mouth-feel of wine that had a certain astringency due to the wine-making methods of the dark ages. Its tendency to dry out the palate likely gave rise to the term "dry wine."

Ironically, the different varieties of grapes don't have uniform tastes! You just can't tell what exact flavors a wine will give you merely by looking at the grapes from which it is made. All grape varieties change their tastes depending on the climate and the soil in which they grow. That's right: what matters most is location, location, location! So geography is everything in wine tasting, and experts are completely familiar with how different grape varieties respond to the various regions where they are grown. The great wine taster is a geographer of wine-growing regions. (More about geography in the next chapter.)

And, of course, rosés don't come from a marriage between whites and reds. Grapes are either red or white (green, actually), and no hybrid grape creates rose-colored wine. So how did it get here? Leave it to the French to discover that they could add a little red wine to a white wine and create rosé. Lately this kind of "cheating" has fallen out of favor, and the common practice is to make rosé wines purely from red grapes.

How can you get rosé wine from a red grape? It takes skill and timing. It may surprise you to learn that the juice of a red grape is the same color as the juice of a white grape; only the skins differ in color. Red wine picks up the color of the skins during processing because the winemaker lets the juice sit together with the skins. This also releases tannins, those dark, tea-like compounds that give a red wine its "dry" feeling. To make rosé wine, the winemaker lets the juice stay with the skins for less time.

SWEET ISLAND: HOW SWEET IT IS – OR ISN'T!

THE WORST WAY TO MAKE a wine sweet is to put sugar in it. This is how most Kiddush wines are made, and like most American Jews, I grew up with a weekly dose of sweet Kiddush wine. When I found out that this wine was considered bad by wine connoisseurs, I lost interest in sweet wines. I started out on my path as a wine taster thinking that the important wines are all dry wines, and that sweet wines aren't particularly noteworthy. Moreover, I was interested in dry wines because I was drawn to the challenge of learning to understand and appreciate them. It took me time to discover that sweet wines can be every bit as amazing as the dry ones. In fact, the most expensive and exclusive wines in the world are sweet ones!

Sweet wines are generally white wines, and they're not sweet from added sugar. A good, natural way to make a sweet wine is to start with grapes that have more sugar in them to begin with. Then when the fermentation process stops, you are left with a sweet wine. White grapes tend to have more sugar in them, but that is not enough to give you a sweet wine. A sweet wine needs a high concentration of sugar in the juice of the grapes. There are several tricks of the trade a vintner can use to concentrate the juice in his grapes. He can leave the grapes on the vine until the sun dries them out somewhat. (That's called a "late harvest" wine.) In colder climates, he can leave the grapes on the vine until they freeze with the first winter snow. This extracts water from the grapes, resulting in a more concentrated, sweeter juice.

Another way of making a sweet wine is intentionally to let a specific fungus called "noble rot" attack the grapes. The fungus sucks out the water, as it changes the chemical makeup of the grapes. This is probably more information than you bargained for. It may not be pleasant to ponder, but the fact is that the sweet wines made from these "rotten" grapes can be truly extraordinary, and are very expensive and sought after. They're pricey because – let's face it – mold is mold. It is not well behaved. If things don't go just right, the vintner might end up with just a bunch of rotten grapes. So when a good wine is produced by this process it is truly special.

As you can see, making a luscious sweet wine is a complex, tedious, and unpredictable process. Another way to make a wine sweet is by fortification – putting some hard alcohol into it, before it is fully fermented. This kills the yeast before it gets a chance to eat up all the sugar. Such wines can be made from red grapes too.

▲ Grapes from Teperberg Winery

A Unique Sweet Wine

Konditon was a popular drink in the Roman Empire, which favored heavily sweetened wines. The Romans left us a cookbook, ascribed to one Apicius, which explains at some length how to make a wine concoction called Conditum Paradoxum (Konditon's Latin name) using generous amounts of honey and dates along with ground pepper, mastic (a kind of spicy sweet tree sap), saffron, and laurel leaves. The word conditum refers to the fragrant spicy sweet taste. The word paradoxum means "surprising" or "paradoxical"; I surmise that the mixture of the honey and pepper gave it a surprising taste, something rather like Yerushalmi noodle kugel, which also is made with caramelized sugar and ground black pepper.

I have always been fond of an Israeli sweet wine called Konditon, put out by Hacormim Winery. According to the label, this wine is based upon an ancient recipe handed down for generations. Besides being very sweet and spicy, it has a distinctive caramel flavor. I have often wondered if this is the original Konditon mentioned in the Talmud!

Eventually contact was made with Eli Shor, a descendant of the pioneer wine-making family that runs Hacormim Winery. He wasn't willing to discuss the blend of spices that goes into their Konditon wine. However, he did say that once the spiced wine was aged in oak barrels, those barrels could convey the same flavor to subsequent vintages on their own. So if you open a bottle of Konditon, the caramel flavor you get is most likely nothing more than the flavor of the grapes, combined with the effects of aging. The wine's sweetness is not the result of any added honey or sugar (as in the Roman Conditum). It comes from several unique varieties of sweet grapes (called Gindly, Damdamoun, and Bayedouni) that grow only in the area of Hebron, the city of the Patriarchs.

SPARKLING ISLAND: WHO PUT THE SPARK IN SPARKLING WINES?

SPARKLING WINES are a challenge to make, unless you use the cheapo seltzer method and pump CO_2 into a wine. That will make it fizz, all right, but like adding sugar, this method is unnatural and demeaning to the wine. A real sparkling wine is made when a second fermentation takes place in the bottle. In the Champagne region of France such "in the bottle fermentations" used to happen by accident. The locals thought this was terrible and they spent lots of time and energy trying to stop it from happening. One day, somebody discovered that bubbly wines are sensational. Voilà! Champagne was born.

If you have a notion to create your own wine, just be careful of one thing. Don't dare make a bubbly wine just anywhere in France and call it Champagne, or you will be arrested and sent to Devil's Island for the rest of your life. Of course, I'm exaggerating a bit. But it is true that the French are fanatical about protecting the rights of each wine-making region. Only wines originating in the Champagne region have the right to be called Champagne. Bordeaux always comes from Bordeaux; Burgundy always comes from Burgundy. It's the law.

When we think of Champagne or sparkling wines in general, we think of white wine. Most sparkling wines are whites, but logically it does not have to be this way. Lately, there are some fine sparkling red wines being produced, some with varying degrees of sweetness. So, on my map, Sparkling Island is colonized by pretty much everybody.

Of the three islands we've discussed, Dry Island is still my favorite place. I love dry wines. Dry wines are what most grapes naturally produce and they can have an amazing array of tastes and aromas. They can be fruity, spicy, earthy, woody – even sweet, in a dry sort of way. Dry wines have a zest and vitality that energize me.

A WORD ABOUT VARIETALS AND BLENDS

MOST OF THE WINES we've been talking about are known as varietals. A varietal is a wine that is made from only one kind of grape, or that has just a little bit of another wine mixed in. Others are a blend of two or more varieties.

How can you tell whether a wine is a varietal or a blend? If a wine is identified on the bottle by the name of a grape, such as Chardonnay or Merlot, that wine is a varietal. On the other hand, you may encounter a wine label that just says "red dry wine" or "red wine" or "table wine." If you check the back label, you will usually find that it is a blended wine. The vintner has combined different wines to create a balanced – and hopefully delightful – effect.

A blended wine is in no way inferior to a varietal; in fact, blending different varieties can be a true enhancement. There are different ways to make great wine, and that's what gives wine making such fascinating, endless possibilities. A Bordeaux wine

(from the French region of Bordeaux) is a blend of any number of five grapes: Cabernet Sauvignon, Merlot, Cabret Franc, Malbec, and Petit Verdot. A common Bordeaux blend is 70 percent Cabernet Sauvignon, 15 percent Merlot, and 15 percent Cab Franc. In contrast, wines from Burgundy are likely to be made only of one variety of grapes. It may be a red Pinot Noir or Gamay, or a white Chardonnay or Pinot Blanc. Some Burgundy wines are made from only one kind of grape grown in a single vineyard. Such wines are called, not surprisingly, "single vineyard wines."

These days, varietals and single vineyard wines are rising in popularity the world over. A blended wine will give you more complexity, and let the different tastes, aromas, and sensations express themselves, but its central body may have a rather indefinite character. In contrast, a varietal – especially a regional or single vineyard wine – will have a powerful central body that can sometimes blow you away, though it may obscure more subtle qualities.

I happen to prefer a good blend to a single vineyard varietal. I like the freer feeling and the interplay between the subtle qualities. But some people love to feel the rush of that powerful taste coming right at them. It is all a matter of personal taste.

Of course, my map of the World of Wine

is greatly lacking in detail; it is up to you to fill in your own map as you continue exploring. With time, you will also develop a geographic map (of real places, not imaginary ones!) where you will locate the wines you appreciate most. The maps of most wine experts strongly emphasize areas in France, Italy, Germany, California, New Zealand, and even South Africa, to name a few, and we will tour these places in the next chapter. Today, some of the finest wineries

are involved in kosher production runs, so Jews like me (who look for reliable rabbinic certification) might yet end up becoming more familiar with these classic wine-making regions in all parts of the globe.

Yet for us the map of Israel looms very large – especially the Golan region, where some of its finest grapes are cultivated. As this small country is a microcosm of the whole world, we will certainly find that all the sensations and qualities one could hope for are there, waiting to be discovered.

Let me share with you a famous story concerning maps. Once, a city fellow went to visit the great Jewish sage the Chofetz Chaim, in the village of Radin in Lithuania. He had brought along a map, which caught the Chofetz Chaim's interest. The visitor explained that a point on the map meant a big important city, that a large dot on the map meant a huge metropolis, and that a star stood for the capital city of a whole nation. When the Chofetz Chaim looked for Radin on the map, it could not be found. Undismayed, he told his visitor that in heaven they also have a map, with points, dots, and stars, indicating the strength of Torah in different places. On that map Radin is a star – and who knows if Berlin, Paris, and London even show up as points? As appreciators of kosher wine, we will end up with our own unique map of the world, and Israel will most certainly be its star.

▲ Vineyards of Bazelet HaGolan Winery, Golan Heights

CHAPTER FOUR

Jewish Geography

Now that we know a little bit about which grapes are used in wine making, it's time to zero in on where these delightful fruits are grown and turned into fine kosher wines. As I hinted earlier, the location of the vineyard (called *terroir* among wine buffs, so you may as well learn the word) plays a role in what kinds of grapes will thrive there and contributes to the unique qualities that can be tasted in the wine. It's hard to define *terroir* in English, so hard that *The Oxford Companion to Wine* sort of gives up, stating apologetically that it is "a French concept."

THE CLOSEST WE CAN come is to say that *terroir* includes the total environment: soil type (composition, nature, fertility, drainage, and ability to retain heat); topography (mountains, valleys, and bodies of water influence how the climate affects the region); and the weather conditions common to the area. Grape growers even calculate the effect of "microclimates" in small areas of land *within* the vineyard. For example, in a lake region where winter weather may be severe, certain varieties of grapes will be planted nearer to the lake, where the air will be a bit warmer, while the hardier varieties

will be planted further away from the lake. While some downplay the role of location, the French (being French) feel that it's the winemaker's mission to bring out the best that a particular *terroir* can produce, so you will see considerable detail on French wine labels about precisely where the grapes you are about to consume were grown.

Where in the world is kosher wine produced? Everywhere! Wineries that are exclusively kosher are emerging all over the globe, and in some cases, non-kosher wineries are complying with kosher certification rules in order to tap into the growing kosher market. Many of these international varieties have a *hechsher* (rabbinic certification) such as OU, OK, or Star-K, and others come with local rabbinic endorsement. Many have both.

So get out your passport! We're going on a worldwide journey to survey some of the top places kosher wines are produced and taste a few of their wines. There's no way to cover them all (it would make a book too heavy to lift), but we can get a picture of what's out there. (At the time of this writing [2011], all of the companies below have known *hechsherim*, but I urge you to look at each bottle before you buy. *Kashrus* is an ever-changing industry.)

Before we leave the American continent, it's important to note that a huge number of wonderful wines are produced right here in the United States. The Royal Wine Corporation operates the Kedem Winery in the Hudson Valley of New York, as well as Herzog Wine Cellars in Oxnard, California, which produces numerous types of wines (some of which have won prestigious awards in international competitions) from nearly a dozen vineyards in the state. The Herzog label also imports a good many wines, but we'll get to that later. Another California producer is Hagafen Cellars, which bottles Cabernet Sauvignon, Chardonnay, Pinot Noir, and Zinfandel, among other wines, in the Napa Valley. The Joseph Zakon Winery bottles Kesser wine from the Long Island region of New York. Perhaps the smallest kosher winery in the United States is Four Gates in the Santa Cruz Mountains of California, run by one man who oversees both the organic growing of the grapes and the making of Chardonnay, Merlot, Pinot Noir, and Cabernet Blanc. I guess you would call this the ultimate of "estate bottling," where the wine is made from grapes grown on the winery's own grounds. New York has a small winery too: Red Fern Cellars on Long Island, which produces Merlot, Cabernet Sauvignon, Chardonnay, and Syrah.

These tiny wineries and their products are sometimes dubbed "boutique" because they make only a limited number of bottles (according to some classifications, less than two thousand cases per year; according to others, five thousand cases). The idea behind a boutique wine (which – just to confuse you – can be made in limited quantity by a big wine producer

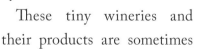
◀ Bordeaux region

too) is that the winemaker has a passion for a specific type of grape or blend of grapes, and wants to try new techniques to make that wine a little different.

You have to know that winegrowers and winemakers regard their occupation as far more than agriculture or manufacture. Viticulture is an art! So when a winemaker decides to experiment, he's doing so with a sense of creativity and adventure, like a painter who wants to fashion something no one else has ever done. The result will not be to everyone's taste, but there will be some people who will share the winemaker's ecstasy about his special wine. If you find yourself sharing the taste of a particular boutique winemaker, you may well decide that it's worth the extra cost to buy his bottles. The fact is that some are quite reasonably priced too.

A TOUR AROUND THE WORLD

NOW LET'S VISIT some other countries and find their kosher wineries. Set your compass, we're going south. First stop, the Alfasi Winery in Chile, just south of Santiago. It's a good place to stock up on Cabernet Sauvignon, Merlot, Syrah, and Chardonnay. We can stop at the Lan Zur and Ha Sod kosher wineries situated in the Lontué Valley not far away to enjoy their Cabernet Sauvignon, Chardonnay, and Rosé wines.

Not too far away, in the cool, dry foothills of the Andes Mountains in the Mendoza province of Argentina, is the Don Guillermo de Mendoza Winery, producing Malbec (dry red) and Cabernet Sauvignon wines.

Andes Mountains

Hopping over the Atlantic to South Africa, we stop in the Paarl Mountain region (not too far from Cape Town), which is known as the capital of the wine-making industry in South Africa. We call on Backsberg Winery to sample their Chardonnay, and Zandwijk Wines, which produces kosher wines under the Kleine Draken label. Quite proud of their homegrown grapes, South African wineries produce a variety of wines that are internationally available.

Heading north to Europe, we stop first in Italy, where roughly a dozen fine kosher winemakers practice their art. Cantina Gabriele has a wide variety of wines including sparkling wines, whites, and reds. Let's try their popular Dolcemente, a combination of Cabernet and Cesanese grapes from an area

called Lazio. While in that central Italian locale, we can try a wine from Tuscany called Toscano Rosso put out by Cantine del Borgo Reale, which also produces a number of other wines from other parts of the country.

Sentieri Ebraici means "paths of the Jew," and this company in the Le Marche region of central Italy states that Jews have been making wine and growing olives in the area since

antiquity. If you think their label resembles a *ketubah* (Jewish marriage certificate), you're right.[1] It takes its design from an Italian *ketubah* dating back more than 260 years. They are obviously proud of a long heritage, which is expressed in several ways. Del Vecchio and Azariah are two robust red wines named for famous Italian rabbis, and a light white wine is named in honor of Dona Gracia Nasi, the sixteenth-century Jewish benefactress who fought to protect persecuted Jews of that era.

Known for its sparkling wines north of Venice, the Bellenda Winery produces *Prosecco Kosher*, made from grapes grown in the Vittoria Veneto region. Of course, no survey of Italian kosher wines would be complete without mentioning Rashi and Bartenura, bottled in numerous places, and imported to the United States by the Royal Wine Corporation. We can stop in the Asti district of northern Italy's Piedmont region, where Moscato grapes are cultivated for Rashi's Moscato d'Asti. Malvasia and other delightful wines are bottled for

[1] To see the *"ketubah"* label, go to http://sentieriebraici.com/wines.php.

◄ Paarl Mountain, South Africa   ▲ Tuscany region, Italy

Bartenura in this area too, though their Chianti is made in Tuscany, where the principal grape (Sangiovese) for this wine is grown.

In the mountainous southeast region of Spain we can taste a lovely red dessert wine called Monastrell Dulce, as well as a beautiful Cabernet Sauvignon, among others. Moving up the Spanish coastline, we reach the slopes of the Montsant region to tour the Cellar de Capçanes, a collective of 120 grape growers which produces wines of high repute, including a kosher brand called Flor de Primavera. (Look for Peraj Ha'abib on the bottle label.) Though the winery has been around for seventy-five years, it undertook the production of kosher wine in 1995 at the behest of the Jewish community of Barcelona, about a hundred miles north. Their kosher wine has been a great success and they are very gratified by this response.

The Herzog company imports a number of wines from France labeled Herzog Selection,

so let's cross the border into France, stopping first in Languedoc, where the Herzog Selection Valflore is made. In Western Languedoc, we also find the home of some fine Abarbanel wines, specifically Merlot (red and white), Cabernet Sauvignon, Chardonnay, Syrah, and a surprising White Shiraz. The vineyards in this area thrive between the Aude River to the east, the Mediterranean Sea to the south, and mountains to the west. (It's a *terroir* thing!)

Going north and east, we come to the Bordeaux region, where numerous Herzog Selection wines are made. A small area in the region called Haut Médoc is the home of their Barons Edmund and Benjamin de Rothschild label, whose blend of Cabernet Sauvignon and Merlot (2003) won prestigious awards.

Since we're in France, where they are *très* sensitive about everything wine, we might as well learn the term *appellation*. Simply put, it is a legally defined and protected geographical indication of a wine-growing region. Côtes du Rhône, for example, is the official Appellation d'Origine Contrôlée (AOC) for the Rhone wine region of France, which may be used by wines bottled throughout the region, though it's more complicated than that. You'll have to talk to a Frenchman to get it straight. To the French, appellation is critical. It will only matter to you if you become a real wine expert to whom the precise location of the field is important.

Traveling northward, we can stop for some Abarbanel Chateau de la Salle red Burgundy from the Beaujolais Villages region. The Chateau de la Salle vineyard has been operated for hundreds of years by the same family and their vines are quite old. Generally speaking, older vines mean better grapes. The entire facility is kosher.

The cold climate of Alsace in northeast France grows the best Riesling and Gewürztraminer grapes. White and sparkling wines dominate this area. (But remember, true Champagne is made only in Champagne, further north and west. I told you the French are touchy about this!) Abarbanel is here too, bottling the above Riesling and Gewürztraminer wine as well as Brut Crémant d'Alsace at the La Cave de Sigolsheim Winery. Abarbanel likes to point out that all of their wines are estate grown and estate bottled, i.e., everything is grown and bottled on the grounds, and even the French government – which, as we know, is picky, picky about this sort of thing – allows them to print that on the label.

Less familiar to the kosher consumer is the Alsace Willm Winery. It, too, produces a fine kosher Gewürztraminer, available in the United States.

Let's stop in Austria at the Hafner Estate Winery, which was established in the thirteenth century – that's right, 1217 to be exact. They have been producing kosher wines since 1980. What is fascinating about this winery is that it's situated near Lake Neusiedl in Burgunland (about twenty-five miles south of Vienna), an area known to Jews since the seventeenth century as the famous Sheva Kehillos, which included Eisenstadt, Mattersburg, and Deutschkreuts (Tzeilem). Hafner is quite enthusiastic about its line of fifty kosher products, and takes special pride in their Chardonnay ice wine, the first of its kind in the Jewish world. Ice wine is made from frozen grapes, which gives it a natural sweetness, and theirs won awards in the United States, Canada, England, and Israel.

After this treat, we'll move onward to the Republic of Georgia, where we can sample Alaverdi semi-sweet red wine from the southeastern region of Kakheti. It is not

far from the Greater Caucasus mountain range.

Hold on to your hat, we're flying to Australia, where several kosher winemakers vie for awards each year. You may have enjoyed outstanding wines (such as the blend of Cabernet and Merlot) from Teal Lake Estate or Altoona Hills, situated in the southeastern part of this country. But Western Australia has its claim to viticulture fame too. The coastal region of southwest Australia is home

Hafner Estate near Lake Neusiedl, Austria

to Joseph River Estate, well worth a stop. Typical of a growing trend, the Beckett's Flat boutique winery in the Margaret River region in Western Australia established a kosher division marketed under the label Five Stones. Although this is a single-vineyard winery (of only thirty-five acres), it produces eight different kosher wines! Before we leave down under, let's hop over to South Island of New Zealand, where we can sample Goose Bay Winery's Pinot Noir.

It's time to head to the Land of Israel, but not until we dip down to the southern slopes of the Troodos mountain range of Cyprus, where the boutique Lambouri Winery bottles Ya'in Kafrisin, literally Cyprus Wine – what else? It's a dry red wine made from Cabernet Sauvignon, Grenache Noir, and an indigenous grape known as Mavro. The word is that this is the first kosher wine produced in Cyprus in two thousand years.

COMING HOME

UNDOUBTEDLY, the most remarkable news is that Israel has become a leading manufacturer of sophisticated wines that are earning a sterling reputation the world over. This tiny country is divided into five wine regions, each offering different microclimates, soil, and environments conducive to growing a huge variety of grapes. Going south to north, they are:

- **Negev** – including the Beersheba Valley and the northern Negev plateau

- **Harei Yehudah** (Judean Hills) including the hills of Bethlehem, Hebron, Beth El, and Jerusalem

- **Shimshon** (Samson) – including the Upper Shefela, Gezer, and Latroun

- **Shomron** (Samaria) – including the Carmel mountain range and the Sharon Plains

- **Galil** (Galilee) – including the lower, central, and upper Galilee and the Golan Heights

If you look at the Golan Heights, for example, you will find a convergence of growing factors like nowhere else on the planet: it has a southern Mediterranean climate, high altitude, and volcanic soil with a little clay (good water capacity and good drainage). Within each of these regions, there are numerous subcategories of conditions, each contributing to the success of a particular vine.

Some people say that when they drink wine from Israel, they can virtually taste the sun, soil, and water of the Holy Land. I suspect that has more to do with one's spiritual palate than with physical taste. In any case, to many of us, the very idea that we are drinking wine made from grapes grown in our ancient homeland is enough to add transcendence to the experience. There is a story of a sage in Europe before World War II who used to go to great lengths to order wine from Eretz Yisrael. When it would arrive, he would run to put on his Shabbos clothing before bringing it into his home.

Warning: to many consumers in the Diaspora, seeing Hebrew letters on a label implies that the product inside is kosher, but let the buyer beware! There are many wineries in Israel that are not kosher, so you must look for reliable rabbinic certification.

Fortunately, the seventeen largest wineries in Israel are all kosher, and many of their products are outstanding in quality. And when I say outstanding, I mean The Best, even according to independent judges, not pushovers like you and me.

You have to know a little about wine competitions. There are some competitions where gold medals are generously handed out. While it's nice for a wine to receive such recognition, it is not necessarily that hard to acquire. But there are some competitions that set the standard. In these competitions, there is only one trophy awarded, and it is regarded as higher than a gold medal.

In terms of quality, the competition

that is arguably most recognized is *Decanter* World Wine Awards, organized by *Decanter* magazine in England. With highly professional judges and stringent controls, winning a *Decanter* competition is a real triumph. And that's just what Carmel Winery did: its Kayoumi Single Vineyard Shiraz 2006 won the *Decanter* International Trophy in 2010 in the Red Rhone varietal group, beating nearly eleven thousand wines from forty-one countries! And it's kosher too, which undoubtedly was a real shock to some snooty connoisseurs who still think "kosher" means sweet and syrupy. I wish I had been there.

Numerous other wines from Israel have been taking awards and ribbons all over the world, and why not? It's grown on holy *terroir*!

We could dance all over Israel, tasting wines of every kind from dozens of wineries, but we'll focus on just a few. The oldest were founded way back in the Old Yishuv days. Zion (in Mishor Adumim) was founded by the Shor family in the Old City of Jerusalem in 1848 (see the sidebar "A Proud Family Heritage"); Teperberg (at Kibbutz Tzora, at the

foot of the Jerusalem Mountains) in 1870; and Carmel was founded in 1882 by none other than Baron Edmond de Rothschild in Zichron Ya'akov (south of Haifa) and Rishon LeZion (south of Tel Aviv). Carmel has vineyards all over the country and it's the largest winemaker in Israel. It also has two small wineries close to key vineyards so there is less time between harvest and production. These are the Kayoumi Winery in the Upper Galilee and the Yatir Winery in the northeastern Negev.

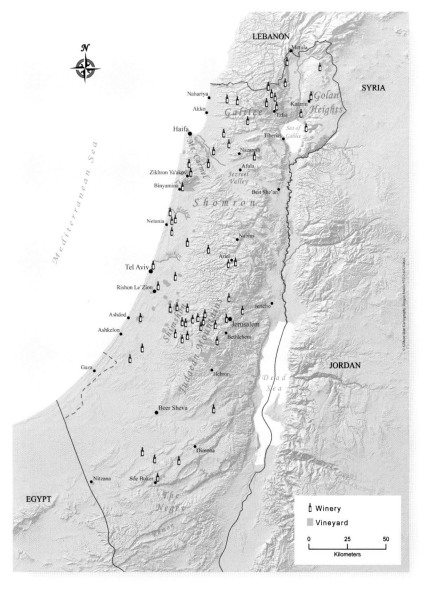

A Proud Family Heritage

The Galin family, originally Karliner Chassidim, came to the Land of Israel from what is now Belarus back in 1835. At the time, there was tremendous expectation and fervor in Europe anticipating the coming Redemption. Many of the students of the Vilna Gaon made their way to Israel, motivated by the belief that 1840 was going to be a pivotal year. Karliner Chassidim were instrumental in rebuilding the Jewish communities of Safed, Tiberias, and Jerusalem. The first member of the Galin family to arrive was Rabbi Mordechai Avraham Galin, who immediately settled in Safed. A few years later, he was appointed *rosh yeshivah* (head) of the Tiferes Israel Yeshiva and moved to the Old City of Jerusalem.

In those days, there was great poverty among the Jews and they lived in cramped quarters in the Old City. Moses Montefiore came to Israel to encourage Jews to supplement their Torah studies with a trade and to build communities outside the Old City walls.

Rabbi Mordechai Avraham and his son, Rabbi Yitzchak, correctly judged that there was demand for wine in the Old City. Yitzchak married the daughter of Jerusalem wine dealer Aaron Shor, taking his wife's surname in order to use the permit issued by Turkish authorities to the Shor family to open a winery. The Shor Brothers Winery opened in 1848. The father and son turned their attention to researching and refining the wine-making processes that were prevalent in Israel at the time. Konditon wine was a result of this painstaking effort.

The winery was situated in a cellar on Haggai Street in the Old City, right next to the Kosel Hama'aravi (Western Wall). It was so close that a section of the Kosel formed the back wall of the cellar, and the workers had to be careful not to lean anything directly against the sacred wall, so as not to defile the holiness of the Temple Mount by mundane use. Empty wine barrels were placed all along the Holy Wall so that forgetful workers would not touch it by mistake!

Shor Brothers Winery operated for more than eighty years. Of all the many small wineries operating in the Old City at this time, only the Shor and Teperberg (today Efrat Winery) families survived ►

▶ as active businesses. They had to leave their Jerusalem cellar, however, in 1925, when the British Mandate authorities ordered all industry out of the Old City. Unintimidated, Shor moved to Beis Yisrael, near Meah Shearim. In the 1940s, a new law ruled that businesses could no longer be known by their family names. Brothers Avraham and Moshe renamed their winery Yikvei Zion, though faithful customers still referred to the winery as Shor.

By 1948, the family and business had grown so much that Moshe and his son, Yitzchak, opened a new plant in Tel Azur (outside Jerusalem) producing mainly spirits. Avraham remained in Beis Yisrael, manufacturing wine and grape juice. The Tel Azur facility eventually split into two, establishing Hacormim Winery in the 1950s.

Throughout this turbulent era, the Shor family played a prominent role in the growth and stability of Jerusalem and Israel. Rabbi Elisha Shor fought in the War of Independence (in a chareidi unit), first in the Haganah and later with the newly formed Israel Defense Forces. Like most Israeli families, they paid in blood for the Jewish state.

In the late 1970s and early '80s, the wineries moved out of Jerusalem to Mishor Adumim (near Maale Adumim), east of Jerusalem, where they continue to produce outstanding wines. Numerous seventh- and eighth-generation members of the family manage this thriving business, continuing a precious tradition.

in red varietals, particularly Cabernet Sauvignon and Merlot.

But let's not overlook the small places. Gush Etzion Winery qualifies as a boutique winery, with a number of products that are organic. Located south of Jerusalem in an area known since ancient times for grape cultivation, the grapes are grown on terraces, taking advantage of the cool, dry climate and chalky soil with good drainage.

Binyamina Winery near Mount Carmel was founded under another name in 1952, and is now the fourth largest winery in Israel. It's a wonderful place to go, especially if you're fond of Shiraz or Merlot.

The wine industry in Israel is comparatively young. With the exception of those already mentioned, most Israeli wineries operating today were established in the 1990s

Central Israel (Hulda) is home to Barkan Winery, the second largest winery in Israel, producing approximately seven to nine million bottles of wine per year. We're talking about eight thousand tons of grapes for this winery alone, brought in from vineyards in the Lachish region, the Galil, Golan Heights, Judean Hills, and Ramat HaNegev. Barkan has adopted the name "Artisans of Red Wine," a well-earned title, as they specialize

Karmei Yosef Winery

and later. They entered a world market that was sometimes hostile to Israeli products and condescending to kosher wines, yet they plugged on, testing the soil, experimenting with different kinds of grapes, and, when necessary, importing wine experts trained in other countries. Eventually, they were ready to enter worldwide competitions, and as a result, Israel is gradually changing its image, emerging as a respected producer of quality wines.

A terrific example of this is the Golan Heights Winery. So put on your hiking boots – we're going way up to Katzrin! Few of us in the Diaspora can fathom the economic importance of the Israeli victory in the Yom Kippur War of 1973, but it's worth the telling.

Picture this: The Golan Heights, an area blessed with ideal growing conditions for grapes, was known as a lush vineyard region in ancient times. Following the bloody battles there in 1973, the area didn't look anything like a fertile vineyard: the ground was littered with burned-out tanks, ammunition, and cannons. But within three years, the land was cleared and precious vines were planted.

By 1983, the first Sauvignon Blanc was produced, and a few years later a permanent winery was built high up in the mountains in the little town of Katzrin. Seven Golan Heights agricultural settlements (and one in the Upper Galilee) partnered in this enterprise, planting Chardonnay and Merlot vines for the first time in Israel. Next, they added Gewürztraminer, Pinot Noir,

Riesling, and other varieties, planting each at an elevation perfect for its cultivation. Hiring top experts in viticulture, the Golan Heights Winery also installed state-of-the-art computerized meteorological instruments that give them precise readings of temperatures, humidity, wind direction and speed, soil temperature, rainfall per hour, and more. Total modernization could not control these conditions, but it certainly gave them an edge in all the decisions that go into everything

from the growing and harvesting of the fruit to the making of wine. And though it sounds like a scientifically controlled mechanism, there was still plenty of room for traditional methods, solid expertise, instinct, and – of course – Divine Providence smiling on the effort.

The Golan Heights Winery started as a tiny experiment with a slim chance of success, and eventually triumphed as a trendsetter with an annual production of more than five million

bottles. You could say that in about fifteen years, it virtually transformed the wine industry in Israel. Nobody expected Israelis to have the sophisticated palates to support this venture, or to pay more for this product. Surprise! Consumers in Israel clamored for it and, indeed, paid more. And when wine from the Heights was exported to other countries, kosher consumers greeted them with the same enthusiasm. The other wine companies in the country took their cue from this "revolution" in fine kosher wine and began developing their own high-quality wines. Kosher boutique wineries blossomed like the flowers on Mount Hermon. And behold, even non-kosher consumers began appreciating Golan Heights wine. Today, a wide variety of wines are bottled under the labels Yarden, Katzrin, Gamla, and Golan. What's more, the Golan region supplies fantastic grapes to wineries all over the country.

That wraps up our brief look at the vast new world of kosher wineries. We've been to Chile, Argentina, South Africa, Italy, Spain, France, Austria, Georgia, Australia, Cyprus, and Israel, and believe me – we've just scratched the surface. But I'll let you in on a little secret: you don't need to go on a global excursion to experience these marvelous wines. Take a few moments looking around your local kosher wine store, and you will discover that all of these exotic wonders are at your fingertips, ready to be tried.

◄ Gush Etzion

Part 2

PRACTICAL
BASICS

CHAPTER FIVE

The Ten Steps of Wine Tasting

The ability to experience wine on a deep level has to be cultivated, like a good vineyard. Have you ever wondered how professional wine critics claim to taste characteristics in wine that are alternately "earthy," "bright," "spicy," "fruity," or "complex"? All that in a little sip of wine?

PREPARATION: DEVELOPING YOUR SENSORY PERCEPTION

YES. IT'S REALLY ALL THERE, but it takes training to identify. Look at it this way: can you tell the difference between store-brand soda and a national brand, or between regular Coke and Diet Coke? Most people can, and that's because they are so familiar with the specific tastes of these drinks that they can easily tell them apart. I've met people

who will drink only Pepsi and not Coke, and vice versa. So you can do this.

One of the few points on which our sages and modern culture agree is that *for anything important, preparation is critical.* For instance, in our holy books, our teachers reveal that *erev Shabbos* (Friday) is the key to a satisfying Shabbos experience, and we have a whole month before Rosh Hashanah to prepare ourselves spiritually. In the physical world, today's fitness experts will tell you that warm-ups before exercising will prevent injuries and make your workout more productive. So before I give you my ten steps of wine tasting, I suggest that you limber up with a few pre-tasting exercises. They will set the tone and help you appreciate what is to come.

Exercise 1: Find the Words

Tasting wine means to experience all the qualities that are rolled up in it. To sense these qualities you have to be able to name them, so you must develop a vocabulary for describing intangible sensations, feelings, and qualities.

I recall a Midrash about Adam in Gan Eden that may be familiar to you. In it, the Creator brought all of the animals to Adam and directed him to name them. To do this, Adam had to feel with all of his superlative senses, his mind, and his heart to answer the question "What is the essence of this creature?" He then summarized his conclusion in a single word, which became the Hebrew designation for that animal. If you look at the

Hebrew names of living creatures, you will find that at their roots they describe a key feature of each one's life or function.

That's what a great wine taster does; and that is what you are going to do. When you sip the wine, your task will be to feel the nature of the wine with as many of your senses as you can. You will see the wine's color, smell its fragrance, taste it with all of your taste buds, and feel its sensation as it goes down. Your heart has to bring all these sensations and feelings together and give them a name. How do you do this?

Sometimes, the right word will pop spontaneously into your mind. Other times, it won't be so quick. When that happens, you have to silence your thoughts, and just feel with your senses. Words and images will come to mind. They are real. You can trust them. Let's say that you are drinking a wine (with sensory awareness) and suddenly a bubbling mountain stream comes to mind. You will hear your heart say "clear, fresh, and sparkly." You might think this comes from your imagination, but its origin is not there. "Clear, fresh, and sparkly" are intangible qualities of the wine. The proof is that when experienced wine tasters get together, each will describe a certain wine in roughly the same words. Each taster may have special terms he or she prefers to use, but overall you will find that the descriptions add up to the same sensation.

So what is the exercise? For the time being, your mission is to get used to feeling sensations and letting your heart give names to them. Let's say you're coming into the kitchen for breakfast. You see the room; you smell its aromas, like the pleasant smell of coffee brewing. You hear the sounds, like the happy noise of your children getting ready for school. Listen, feel, smell…and see what words come into your mind. What is your heart telling you? Do you feel the joy of a new day? Do you sense optimism? Do you savor the delicious smell of a hearty breakfast?

When you go to *shul*, do you encounter the mustiness of aged books, or the streamlined sharpness of an air-conditioned synagogue? Take a few moments in the course of your day, especially when you go from one location to another, to still your mind and give names to the qualities of each place. Let sensations come together in your mind and let your heart supply images, associations, and descriptive words.

This exercise will help add a dimension of richness to your life that is essential if you want to appreciate great wines, but it will also do a good deal more. You will be more aware of your surroundings, more sensitive to everything going on around you. What's more, you will be a more interesting person, because you will be able to share your life experiences in greater detail, with more feeling and with depth. Now when you come home from a day at work, you will have more to share with your family. No more conversations like, "What happened today?" "Nothin' much." So this exercise is good for your relationships too!

Once you feel comfortable naming things, you will be ready for the next exercise.

Exercise 2: Prepare Word Cards

When you start tasting, you may find yourself somewhat stumped over how to name the qualities you encounter in your wine. Fortunately, you don't have to invent an entire wine vocabulary on your own. Wine tasters share their vocabularies with each other. You may want to read wine reviews or look at wine blogs online. Some of them can be pretty boring (and intimidating), but what you are looking for is the descriptive words the tasters use. These can be generalizations, like "dry" and "sweet," or more subtle words like "crisp" or "rich" or "peachy." There might even be more abstract words like "vibrant," "effervescent," or "perfectly balanced."

Zero in on the terms that mean something to you. If you have been naming the feelings in your life for a while, this should be easy for you. Write these words on a card. When you finally do drink your wine, you will have a ready-made collection of words to assist you in understanding and appreciating its qualities. Prepare an aroma card too.

The senses of taste and smell are very closely related. Smell expands the range of taste.

Listen, I won't hold back. Below are my personal Taste and Aroma Cards. But don't rely on my words; your experience will be more satisfying if you come up with your own. Of course, you will be able to throw your cards away once you have gotten some serious wine-tasting experience under your belt.

Aroma Qualities
walnut · tobacco · haystack · chocolate
orange · apple · honey · blackberry
plum · prune · raisin · apricot

Taste Qualities
sweet · sour · bright · dark · light
heavy · dry · tart · earthy · sunny
fruity · spicy · woody · leathery

THE TEN STEPS TO ENJOYING WINE

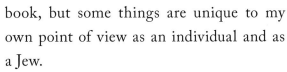

NOW IT'S TIME to put your skills to the test. I have devised the Ten Steps of Wine Tasting. The number is no accident. In Judaism, the number ten symbolizes wholeness and perfection, and that certainly is what we are striving to discover in the wine and in ourselves. Much of what I will say here can be found in any wine-tasting

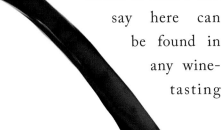

book, but some things are unique to my own point of view as an individual and as a Jew.

Let's get a few things straight. When wine critics approach a wine, they first look for negative qualities such as unpleasant color or aroma. It's their business to take note of the wine's strengths and weaknesses. But if you are new to wine tasting, you shouldn't be trying to judge the wine, just to appreciate it.

Some people tell me that they are put off by wine tasting because it seems too formalized. True! Wine tasters do have special ways of doing things. But that's because these methods work, and I, for one, see no reason to reinvent the wheel. If you want to have a special kind of wine experience, you need to give structure to your wine tasting, instead of doing it haphazardly. Following the steps I've devised will give you four distinct sets of information and experience about the particular wine's qualities:

• *Aroma* (called "nose")

• *Taste*

• *Aftertaste* (called "finish")

• *Color*

My Ten Steps will also help you enjoy your kosher wine in a truly Jewish way. Let's go!

1 CHOOSE THE WINE

One of these days, you will know many different kinds of wine, and you may even have a wine collection of your own. You will then be able to make an informed choice about what wine to taste. For now, you are learning, so you will have to rely on the advice of others to help you choose. Do your homework. Read reviews on the different kosher wines out there. Then go to your local wine store, ask the advice of an expert there too, and then choose a really good, fine wine. Don't scrimp now, because if you try your skills on a poor-quality wine, you will blunt them for good.

Ideally, you should start with wine that is dry, not sweet or bubbly. But if you are used to sweet wines only, you may want to start with a semi-sweet wine. You may find white wines less overpowering than red ones. If you are adventurous, you can try diving right in with a full-bodied, robust red, though it usually takes time to adjust to those. What matters most is that your beginning as a wine taster is based upon a good first wine.

2 SET THE SCENE AND JUST SIT

Choose a tranquil time, and an attractive, tasteful place. Even if you are sitting by yourself, be sure to set up a table, with a white tablecloth. The white will help you see the wine's color. I personally like a bright sunlit room for tasting, since the natural light brings out so much of the wine's color. (But be careful not to put the bottle in direct sunlight, because this can make the wine lose some of its character.) I know some tasters who prefer candlelight. The important thing, of course, is that your surroundings should reflect your tranquil yet focused state of mind. Prepare the scene slowly and deliberately, and you will find your mind becoming more calm and reflective. Prepare your senses to do their work.

Sit for a while. We so often chow down food, grab a cup of coffee, and toss off a text message. Our poor, harried minds are in no position to appreciate subtleties. Let the tensions of the day flow out of your body. Think about the bottle of wine and imagine that it has a secret that it wants to tell, a real "message in a bottle." Breathe deeply and slowly while looking at the beauty of the setup. The glass is crystal clear, and it bends the sunlight streaming in through the window. The bottle is shapely and balanced. Soon a sense of curiosity and anticipation will arise. This is the mood you want to encourage; let it grow.

3 HEAR THE WINE

All of your senses should be involved, including your hearing. Wine has a joyous tinkling sound as it strikes a clear wine glass. Pour the wine gently, but with enough force that it will produce a sound. Listen for it, and let your heart be glad. Fill the wineglass about one-third full.

4 SEE THE WINE

If you tilt the glass a little, the wine will be like water in a swimming pool, with a deep end and a shallow end. If you look through the deep end at the white background of the tablecloth, you will see the wine's robust color. When you look through the shallow end, lighter hues will appear. Let your eyes take in all this beauty. When you swirl the wine in the glass (with circular motions), the upper part of the glass gets coated with a thin film of wine. This film doesn't just sink back into the main body of wine at the bottom of the glass. It spreads to the sides, forming little streams that flow down the insides of the glass. The streams tend to flow in an arch, forming shapes called "legs." What do they say about the wine? Not much, really. The wine critic might make some judgments based upon them concerning the wine's alcohol content, but your purposes are purely aesthetic.

5 SMELL THE WINE

Wine releases its fragrance (what we call bouquet) when you swirl it. In fact, swirling the wine in the glass exposes more of the surface of the wine to the air, bringing out more aroma and flavor. So give the wine a few swirls and sniff the glass. Don't be shy. Thrust your sniffer right into the glass. Don't breathe too deeply. Short sniffs pick up the aromas better. By now, you should be pretty adept at letting your mind take in the sensations as your heart provides names for the qualities they convey. Now you have involved three of your five senses, so you can name some qualities you have encountered.

6 RECITE THE BLESSING

Since wine is very special in Jewish law, it merits a special blessing, *borei pri hagafen*, which thanks G-d as the Creator of the fruit of the vine. Reflect on the fact that the wine did not get here by accident. G-d has given you this wonderful opportunity to explore and appreciate His world. Say the blessing and let the gratitude well up in your heart!

7 DRINK THE WINE AND SENSE ITS SUBTLETIES

Wine tasters do all sorts of things to bring out the full range of a wine's tastes and aromas. They swish the wine around in their mouths to ensure that it reaches all surfaces of the tongue. Some wine tasters know a way of drawing air into their mouths while the wine is there. Some make sure to gently slurp their second mouthful of wine, but not their first. As for myself, I never managed the air-sucking trick without dribbling all over my shirt, and my mother always warned me that it's not nice to slurp. So I forgo those techniques.

However, getting the wine all over the inside of your mouth is very important. Different areas of the tongue sense different tastes, and they all have to be in on the action. So you should definitely swish the wine around inside your mouth. There are actually two different tastes a wine gives you. The first you get when the wine is on your tongue. The second comes on as you swallow, and it's called the finish. These tastes are often quite different, and you should pay attention to both of them. If you breathe out through your nose right after you swallow, you better release the wine's "second taste." In some wines, you will find that the finish changes over the course of a few seconds. Unexpected flavors may start popping like fireworks. Use your Taste Card to alert you to some of these qualities. It's very possible that other words will come to mind too.

As you swish and swallow, pay attention to the actual feeling of the wine in your mouth and throat. This adds the sense of touch to your wine tasting, and completes the use of your five senses. All of them now have been brought into the wine-tasting experience. You have seen the wine, heard it, smelled it, tasted it, and touched it. But you're not finished yet.

8. FEEL THE WINE INSIDE YOU

Other wine-tasting guides won't bother to tell you to do this, and I suppose that if I weren't an observant Jew, I wouldn't have taken note of it either. But I take my cue from Psalms (105:15): "He [G-d] causes vegetation to sprout for the animal, and plants through man's labor, to bring forth bread from the earth; *and wine that gladdens man's heart...and bread that sustains the heart of man.*" From this verse, we see that "gladdening" and "sustaining" are closely related. In this amazing world, G-d has given wine to help us feel fulfilled.

I'm not shy about drinking a hearty amount of wine, and I enjoy the feeling as it settles warmly inside of me. It would be silly to deny that wine is intoxicating; you get an open, expansive feeling, and I appreciate that. Of course, I am always careful never to cross the line. Getting drunk destroys the entire experience and turns beauty into ugliness. But a happy high arises naturally along with the wine's more subtle qualities.

Some wine tasters advocate avoiding intoxication by spitting out the wine instead of swallowing it. (Special tasting rooms at wineries accommodate this practice.) This makes it possible for them to taste many different wines at a long sitting. As a Jew, I think this is wasteful. We are commanded not to toss away the good things we have been given, and not to destroy food needlessly. We should have reverence for the bounty we have. If there is no place for it in my body, I won't drink it.

9 DESCRIBE THE EXPERIENCE

Here is where the skills you developed in giving names to feelings and qualities come to the fore. Now you have the wine's impressions fresh in your mind. Try to describe the wine's many qualities. The more descriptions you come up with, the more discerning you will become. The more discerning you become, the more qualities you will find at your next wine tasting. This ability develops until you become a truly savvy and sensitive wine taster. Many wine tasters keep a notebook handy to write down for future reference the words and names that come to mind.

10 RECITE THE FINAL BLESSING

There is an abbreviated Grace after Meals especially designed to be recited after drinking wine. In order to say this blessing, you need to drink an amount known as a *revi'is,* about 3.3 fluid ounces. In ancient times, the *revi'is* was considered to be the perfect quantity of wine for drinking, and was usually consumed in two consecutive sips. I suspect that when you fill your wine glass one-third to one-half full, you are pretty much approximating the *revi'is* of yesteryear. However, we tend to take smaller sips, over a longer period of time, so I often find myself wondering whether I am eligible to recite that Final Blessing. The blessing is important to me, because the attitude of thankfulness is, to my mind, an integral part of the wine tasting. And this blessing expresses thankfulness along with our love for the Land of Israel, our hopes for Redemption, and our yearning for a peaceful world. So at the end of my wine tasting, I take two final swallows of the wine, more quickly than if I were just tasting it. That way, I'm sure I am allowed to recite the blessing. The text for this Final Blessing can be found in any prayer book and most Grace after Meals booklets. If you drink a wine of the Land of Israel, the text changes a little at the end, so pay attention.

Those are my Ten Steps of Wine Tasting. When I go through them, I feel enriched and renewed physically, emotionally, and spiritually. Wine tasting is a celebration of life and of the incredible variety of beauty in this world. After a wine tasting, I can return to the rush of modern life as a more tranquil, uplifted, and sensitive person. That alone is worth everything. Try it and I am sure you will agree.

Gvaot Winery

ASSESSING YOUR WINE-TASTING EXPERIENCES

AFTER YOU HAVE practiced a little, you should be picking up on the subtle tastes and aromas. If you are not, in all probability you're drinking a mediocre wine. Don't tell yourself, "Oh, it must be my lack of good taste!" Instead, try a different (and hopefully better) wine. It's also a good idea to aerate the wine before drinking it. You may consider purchasing an aerator (a fairly simple and inexpensive gadget through which wine is poured to mix air into the wine) to improve the taste of full-bodied wines. When it comes to quality, I find that wines fall into four categories: bad, okay, good, and great. Let's see how this works.

A bad wine gives unpleasant experiences. Well, it's true that sometimes you have a bad sweet wine that doesn't give you a totally nasty jolt, because a whole bunch of sugar was dumped into it. But it will sure give you a stomachache if you have too much.

An okay wine is drinkable. It goes down your throat. But I don't quite see the point in drinking it when your favorite soft drink is cheaper – unless you are a *yeshivah bochur* on Purim with a tight budget.

A good wine gives you some subtle pleasure, and as you drink it you will find a word or an association arising in your mind. You will smell it, and you might find yourself saying "Hmm, this reminds me of a plum orchard!" Then you will sip it, and sure enough, it still reminds you of a plum orchard. After you

swallow it, the plum orchard is still there. It's probably a nice enough wine and you've discovered a new pleasure. The problem with this wine is that it is "one dimensional." So give that winery a *yasher koach* for being on the right track. Watch for next year's vintage; it may be much better.

Are you ready for a great wine? That is one that brings you lots of subtle qualities in its taste and aroma. You don't get just one association or word rising in your mind, you get several. And when you take more sniffs and more sips, more qualities come out to play with your senses. A wine that does this is said to have "complexity." The grapes have encoded in their chemical makeup diverse nuances from the environment in which they grew. The wine from those grapes brings you these nuances in the form of tastes and aromas. Interestingly, sometimes a taste or aroma might not be pleasant in itself, but the wine will still be a great wine. This is because the wine is communicating something interesting, and because the other qualities of the wine balance everything out. A wine like this is all the more enjoyable because of the skillful balancing act it performs.

This need for balance is especially common in dry red wines, especially those made from the Cabernet Sauvignon grape. Red grapes contain a substance called tannins, found in the skins and seeds. Tannins taste something like unsweetened dark tea. They have an acidic taste that makes your mouth pucker up and go dry. In fact, tannins are often responsible for a dry wine being dry![1] They don't taste that good, but they are an important element of the wine's overall flavor. If the tannins are balanced out by the other tastes and aromas, they give the wine a wonderful, serious attitude and a solid, hearty quality. If they are a little bolder, they make the wine rugged and down to earth, something you might call a manly wine. But if the tannins get out of control, watch out! The wine might not be even drinkable.

Similarly, there are some very fine white wines made from Riesling grapes which actually have a petrol taste or aroma. Many people don't like this taste, and you can understand why. However, wine lovers think well of it, because it contributes to a wine's complexity. When you have the petrol taste balanced out by the fruity flavors of a wine, it is an amazing combination. Imagine the excitement you get from watching a tight-rope walker balancing over a canyon, sidestepping disaster with every step and even making it look easy! A great, well-balanced wine can be like that. One of the qualities might have some bite to it, but the balancing act saves the day.

[1] The other cause of a dry taste is when yeast converts all of the sugar in a wine to alcohol.

An obvious analogy suggests itself. The incense that was once offered in our Holy Temple in ancient Israel was composed of eleven different kinds of resins, perfumes, and spices, all ground to a fine powder and combined in perfect balance and harmony. One of the substances in the incense was called *helbena* in Hebrew (galbanum, a bitter aromatic gum resin). It actually smelled bad. But combined with everything else, it added something to the complexity of the final aroma, and presumably to the spiritual effect of the offering!

A CLEAR CHOICE

THE RIGHT WINEGLASSES can really boost your wine-tasting experience and help you appreciate the beauty of wine. You have certainly noticed that some wineglasses are rounder, some elongated; some have wider rims, others are tapered. The shape of a wineglass is based on more than simple good looks. Each is designed to capture and enhance the aromas and flavors of specific types of wines, ensuring maximum enjoyment.

It is easier and better to do everything with the right tools. You really should equip yourself with wineglasses that work with the wine, not against it. It need not be a huge investment. The idea is to choose the right glasses for the wines you enjoy, not necessarily the most expensive ones.

Choose wineglasses that are made of good, thin, clear glass, not decorative or colored. Part of the enjoyment of wine is appreciating its color. Anything but a clear glass takes away from appreciating the wine in the glass.

A wineglass is said to have a bowl, a stem, and a foot. The glass stem is not just for aesthetic reasons; it may be held without covering the bowl with fingerprints. (Stemless wine tumblers are growing in popularity because people tend to entertain less formally these days and stemware implies an element of formality. But stemless glasses lose all of the benefits provided by stemmed glasses – as I will soon explain.)

For white wine, you'll want a glass with a small bowl and tall stem; for red wine, choose a larger bowl with a relatively short stem. Now you're asking why, and I don't blame you. Believe me, there's a science to this. In simple terms, white wine is served chilled and therefore should be kept away from the heat of your hand. The small-capacity bowl helps keep the temperature cool for a longer time. Red wine, on the other hand, is best served just a few degrees below room temperature (64°–68°F), so it will release its heady vapors when it is warmed by the body heat in your hand. The wider bowl also lets in more air, which aids in bringing out the bold aromas and flavors that typify red wines.

Even within these general guidelines of white wineglasses and red wineglasses, there are even finer gradations. If you are a real connoisseur, you will want a wider, shallower glass for your white Chardonnay, because it is enhanced by more oxidation, like a red wine. The other white wines benefit from having less air exposed to the wine's surface, as that preserves their clean, crisp flavor. Within the red wine category, Bordeaux glasses are tall and broad, allowing full-bodied wines such as Cabernet Sauvignon and Syrah to reach the back of the mouth sooner (to be better enjoyed by the taste buds there). Burgundy glasses are broad, with a big bowl to allow more aromas to surface in the delicate reds, such as Pinot Noir. The shape of the glass also directs the wine more to the tip of your tongue, where the taste buds best suited to that wine are waiting.

Then there are those long-stemmed, thin Champagne flutes with a small mouth used for sparkling Champagne and Asti Spumante. That long, narrow bowl helps retain the carbonation, which keeps your sparkling wine bubbly, and also enhances the visual effect of the wine. Doesn't it look lovely in the glass, with all those bubbles rising?

Of course, if you plan to use several types of wine, but don't want to shell out for wine-specific stemware, buy the generic tulip-shaped wineglasses. They are a sort of compromise genre that will accommodate most wines, or at least, not negate their qualities.

By the way, it's best to hand wash your glasses with plain warm water, as soap can build up inside the glass and affect the wine's flavor.

We will not discuss plastic. I'm no snob, but if someone hands me wine in a plastic cup, I regard it as soda and drink it accordingly.

A Glass Act

I was visiting a good friend in Israel, when he opened a bottle of wine that he had purchased at a local grocery store. He poured some for me and some for himself into regular water glasses. After we drank, he commented, "You know all this stuff you are supposed to sense in the wine – all these aromas and tastes and whatnot. I just don't get it. I drink this stuff and it's okay. I mean, it goes down my throat all right. But it just tastes like dry red wine to me. There are no 'full body,' 'fruity,' or 'spicy' flavors that you often talk about."

"Well," I said, "the first thing you should notice is that you're not using wineglasses."

"You actually mean to tell me it makes a difference?"

"Absolutely! The shape of the glass brings together the aromas so your nose can sense them. If you don't taste with your nose, you are just not getting it. Your tongue only senses four kinds of tastes: salty, sweet, sour, and bitter. The rest of your taste experience is supplied by your nose. That's why nothing tastes good when you have a cold with a stuffy nose."

"So let's try these glasses!" he challenged, producing a nice pair of wineglasses.

"Those look good," I said. He poured the wine. I showed him how to swirl the wine in the glass to release its fragrances. We sniffed the wine. Then we drank. He looked disappointed.

"It's just the same," he concluded. "All I taste is this boring dry wine taste. I didn't smell anything."

"Try again. Clear your mind and sniff. Now, what do you smell?"

"Hey, I'm getting it!" he shouted. "I do smell something! It smells like…like…lighter fluid!"

"And what does that say about the wine?" I asked.

"It's not very good, right?"

"Now you know! The reason you don't get good experiences out of your wine is not just because you didn't use the right glasses. You need real wine to put in those glasses too. The stuff you are drinking is just not quality wine. As you say, it goes down the gullet, but that's about it. This wine has almost no character of any kind. No wonder you're not having any of the exquisite experiences that wine tasting should give you! By the way, how much did you pay for this bottle of joy?"

"Oh, about twenty-five shekels" (roughly seven dollars in US currency).

"Well, buddy," I smiled, "here's the good news. You're getting more than your money's worth! In fact, the wine was quite good for its price, but don't expect to get great pleasure from it. I think you're due for an upgrade – and keep those real wineglasses handy."

CHAPTER SIX

Understanding Dry

Let's assume you enjoy sipping a good sweet wine, and you want to move on to appreciating dry wines, but you're having trouble making the transition. Or to put it in terms of my Wine Map, you have bravely set sail from Sweet Island, but you're encountering navigational problems on the way to Dry Island.

YOU MAY FIND that dry wine just doesn't awaken your senses, or that the tastes and aromas you're experiencing are unpleasant. Maybe it just smells weird and tastes funny to you. If you have been trying bottles of highly recommended wine, you should be experiencing something good, right?

Don't be frustrated. I could just tell you to be patient, that in time you will acquire the taste buds and a sophisticated palate.

I could emphasize that whatever is worth doing takes time. That is all true. But I would like to go farther than that and give you something to think about.

Shiki Rauchberger, Teperberg Winery

MIND GAMES

YOU DON'T JUST taste with your tongue. You taste with your mind, too. You see, the way we perceive things – the way we see, hear, smell, taste, and feel the world around us has a lot to do with the preconceived ideas in our heads. We never just look at things. Based on previous events or sensations, our minds are constantly interpreting our experiences before we even know we are having them! You can see how true this is by looking at the ambiguous images below. An ambiguous image is one that can be seen in two or more ways. Here is one you have probably seen before.

What do you make of this? Is it a vase or two faces? Do you see how changing your idea about the image changes your perception of it?

How about this next one?

You see a certain type of animal. Nevertheless, there is another way of looking at the picture that will turn it into something else altogether. This second way of seeing might be difficult to find. Relax your mind and your eyes, and let yourself lose focus on the image. Don't work at figuring it out. Now you might notice things shifting about in the image. The emphasis may move this way and that. And then, something will emerge that you didn't see before.

Depending whether your brain first interpreted the left side of the picture as a bill or as ears, you saw either a duck or a rabbit. Looking at it the other way changes the duck into a rabbit or the rabbit into a duck.

So what does this have to do with wine tasting? Everything! Right now, as you try to get into dry wines, your nose and your taste buds are receiving sensations that they might not have had before. Your mind doesn't know how to interpret and understand these new sensations. It might very well be that you're drinking great wine, but your mind has no idea what to make of it. It's stuck on one perception and can't comprehend it any other way. It's like seeing the ambiguous image only one way.

Something has to shift, but your brain has not made that shift yet. I would like to introduce you to a little idea that I think can help you discover a new way of tasting. You may be surprised to find that it is a spiritual, Torah-oriented concept. I call it "turning the grape inside out."

A BRIEF PHILOSOPHIC *DRASHAH*

A GRAPE IS SWEET and fruity. But all over the outside of the grape is a naturally occurring yeast whose sole purpose is to turn all the sugar in the grape into something else in order to make it wine. What "something else" is that? Alcohol. Grapes can rot or shrivel into raisins, but the alcohol in wine transforms the grape into something eternal. Though wine can eventually turn into vinegar, it lasts much longer than a plain grape.

Isn't that how G-d transforms us through our keeping the *mitzvos* in His Torah? He takes us from being frail, material creatures and gives us a share in eternity! And just as alcohol is combustible, bursting into flames under the right conditions, we "burst" with renewed vigor and sense of purpose when we do a *mitzvah*, for we are concentrating our energies in the service of goodness and eternal truths.

The grape is no longer sweet, but instead it has become so much more. I think of the grape as being reversed, or turned inside out. The taste of the grape is still there, but rather than expressing itself in qualities of sweetness, it manifests itself in the opposite way – through qualities of tartness, sourness, or even bitterness. These might not sound like appealing qualities, but I assure you that there is no reason why they can't be delicious in their own way. They are the grape's sweetness turned inside out, giving us the benefit of this maturing process!

Dry wine is not meant to immediately delight your senses like candy. The taste of the grape "turned inside out" is not sweet in a material way. It is invigorating and energetic in a spiritual way. It is refined and meaningful. To my mind, appreciating it brings us closer to developing true holiness and to sensing the kind of experience we will have in the Messianic World to Come.

In any event, the mental image of the grape turned inside out gives me a good way of conceptualizing the taste of dry wine. To get the concept is to get the taste. We have said that a good wine has the quality of complexity, which means that several different sensations are wrapped up in it harmoniously. That is one of the wonders of wine. But there should be a central feature, a "body" of the wine that holds it all together. Conceptualizing the inside-out grape also helps me locate the body. You don't have to be a natural-born wine detective; locating and sensing the body of a wine is one of the skills you can cultivate.

So set your sails again, and this time, steer straight for Dry Island. *Bon voyage!*

CHAPTER SEVEN

How to Navigate a Wine Menu in a Restaurant

Most of us aren't exactly thrilled when it comes to ordering wine in a stylish restaurant. Many fear it as a most intimidating and embarrassing moment. If you know little or nothing about wine, you'll easily get confused when given a huge leather-bound wine list after you've placed the order for your meal. The waiter stands patiently as your eyes skim down the list, searching for something you recognize that would suit your taste.

YOU SPOT A WINE you've always enjoyed and look up at him hopefully. The corners of his mouth turn down slightly and he responds diplomatically, "As you wish, but may I suggest..." and he points to a completely different varietal. "Hmm," you mutter thoughtfully as your face colors to a rose tint, "that's an even better choice."

You feel you blew it! But take heart. It won't happen again, because with a little know-how, you can start ordering wine with your head held high. A good restaurant should be able to accommodate all levels of wine drinkers, from beginners to aficionados. There's no shame in asking for recommendations from the *sommelier*; he is trained to know what wine will complement the meal you've ordered. But I'll teach you the basics of wine selection so you won't have to depend on him; it's easier than you think.

The right pairing brings out the best in both the food and the wine. If you are ordering the same meal for everyone, it's a bit easier to base your decision on the main foods in your meal (with perhaps another wine to accompany dessert). If you're dining with a number of people and each has ordered different foods, you might want to order both a red and a white bottle to satisfy everyone; or choose a versatile wine that will go with many food varieties.

If you wonder whether to go by the glass or bottle, remember that it's less expensive to get a bottle if two or more guests are each having a couple of glasses of wine, and you'll be much more limited in your selection when ordering by the glass. Keep in mind that a typical bottle of wine (750 ml) should serve three to four people.

RED WINES

Bin No.		Glass	Bottle
51	**BARON HERZOG** Cabernet Sauvignon (California) *Full bodied yet soft, some fruit overtones, and chocolate aromas*		28
52	**BARON HERZOG** Merlot (California) *Plummy, soft, with an oak bouquet*	8	28
53	**SEGAL'S** Cabernet Sauvignon (Israel) *Rich blackberry and dark cherry flavors, subtle hints of anise and a long finish*	10	36
54	**BARON HERZOG** Syrah (California) *Distinct berry and blackberry fruit notes*		28
55	**RED BY W** (California) *Flavors of blackberry and pomegranate, grenadine and fresh berries with a crisp finish*	8	28
57	**BARTENURA** Chianti (Italy) *A dry, full-bodied wine with appealing berry and spice aromas and a lingering finish*		34
58	**WEINSTOCK CELLAR SELECT** Cabernet Sauvignon (California) *Full bodied with rich blackberry, anise and oak flavors*	13	45
59	**CHATEAU DE LAGRAVE** (France) *Medium-bodied, crisp and dry*		32
60	**HAGAFEN CELLARS** Pinot Noir (California) *Ripe fruity flavors, bright acidity and a clean finish*		60
61	**TEAL LAKE** Shiraz (Australia) *Spicy, fragrant bouquet, soft and dry*	8	28
62	**BARON HERZOG** Zinfandel (California) *Oak bouquet with plum and berry flavors*		28
63	**HAGAFEN CELLARS** Merlot (California) *Plum, coffee, black licorice and oak character*		62
64	**RAMON CORDOVA** Rioja (Spain) *Dark berry, oak and nutmeg aromas with spicy and fruity flavor*	9	30
65	**TEAL LAKE RESERVE** Cabernet Sauvignon (Australia) *Rich currant, black cherry and chocolate flavors with subtle oak nuances in the background*		40
66	**RASHI** Barolo (Italy) 2004 *Dark fruit aromas, dry, and velvety smooth*		7
67	**BARON HERZOG** Pinot Noir (California) 2009 *Flavors of blackberries, cherries and spice, with a soft and smooth finish*	11	8
68	**BARKAN** Merlot Argaman (Israel) 2009 *Dark purple color with fresh fruit aroma, depth, body and tannins, and fresh wild berry flavors*		

An additional consideration is price: decide how much you want to spend and look for wines that are in your price range. You can ask the server for suggestions about a wine in the price range you are considering. They will usually pick up on this clue and not suggest wines out of your budget.

WINE AND FOOD PAIRING – COMMON SENSE OR MYSTERY?

HUNDREDS OF BOOKS and articles have been written on the seemingly mysterious formulae governing food and wine pairing. The experts would like you to think that it is a complicated matter, and that the wrong choice could ruin your meal. So the first thing you should know is that your personal taste comes first. If you like a particular wine, it's not "wrong" to drink it with your meals. Chances are, however, that you are thinking of the taste of that wine when you drink it by itself. You may not realize the specific impact it will have on your taste buds after you've eaten a particular food.

That's where the insider "rules" come in. They are designed to enhance the dining experience for most people. It's some comfort to know that even the experts disagree on the particulars (because, after all, it is a matter of taste), but they do tend to agree on the general principles.

The old rule is that white wine goes with white meat, red wine with red meat. Now, that leaves a lot of gray areas, in my opinion. There are so many foods that are not meat, and even meat can be prepared so many different ways that one rule can't cover them all.

Let's use common sense here. When you're eating a light, simple dish such as roast chicken, you want a light, crisp wine that won't overwhelm the food's mild flavor. (Try a dry Riesling or Champagne, for instance.) But if you've ordered a hearty steak, you want a bold wine that can stand up to it, such as Cabernet Sauvignon. Hot and spicy foods go well with an equally zesty Shiraz, though some people may prefer another fruity red wine with slightly less personality.

Now here's where the nuances come in. Even though food-wine pairing charts will recommend specific wines for broad categories of food, the way the food is prepared is often more important. *Your wine should be matched to the dominant flavor of the dish.*

For example, let's say you've ordered halibut. If it's being served plain without a fancy sauce, Sauvignon Blanc will taste right with it. But if that halibut is served in a rich cream sauce, a Chardonnay would be a better choice – at least according to some people. But you've got to let your own taste buds do the talking.

Below is a list of general principles and some specific pairing suggestions that I've compiled for you. After each food or type of food, I give you the preferred general category of red or white wine (though sometimes both will work), so you will know where to start looking on the menu. That generalization is followed by specific suggestions for which wines would go with that food. Go for the ones you like.

Don't worry. You don't have to memorize this list, and there's no test at the end of this chapter. But before you go to a restaurant, consider beforehand what you might want to order and consult the list to determine which wines are likely to complement that meal. Those wines you should memorize – or at least jot down a few good choices – so you won't feel lost while the waiter is noiselessly tapping his foot.

FOOD-WINE PAIRING SUGGESTIONS

MAIN COURSES

Cream sauce dishes
WHITE WINES: Sauvignon Blanc, Riesling, Chenin Blanc, dry Champagne, Chardonnay

Dishes with tomato sauce
RED WINES: Zinfandel, Barbera, Malbec

Pasta with tomato sauce
RED WINE: Syrah/Shiraz

Sole/Halibut/Salmon/Tuna/Sea Bass
WHITE WINES: Chardonnay, Sauvignon Blanc, Pinot Grigio, Riesling

Smoked salmon
SPARKLING WINES: Brut, Asti Spumante

Chicken
WHITE WINES: Chardonnay, Sauvignon Blanc, Riesling, White Zinfandel, Champagne.
RED WINE: Pinot Noir

Grilled chicken
WHITE WINES: Pinot Grigio, Chardonnay
RED WINE: Cabernet Sauvignon

Turkey
RED WINE: Pinot Noir
WHITE WINE: aged dry Riesling

Beef/veal/duck
RED WINES: Cabernet Sauvignon, Merlot, Syrah/Shiraz, Zinfandel, Barbera, Gamay

Spicy beef/poultry/fish/veal (Sephardic or Asian cooking, for example)
WHITE WINES: Pinot Grigio, Riesling, White Zinfandel.
RED WINES: Shiraz, Cabernet Sauvignon

Lamb
RED WINE: Pinot Noir (Burgundy is French Pinot Noir)

Spicy lamb
RED WINES: Merlot, Cabernet Sauvignon, Syrah/Shiraz

DESSERTS

The general rule is to pair the sweetness (or tartness) of the dessert with the same qualities of the wine. If you match a non-sweet wine with a sweet dessert, the drink will taste bitter in comparison. There is an entire category of dessert wines with varying levels of sweetness on most menus.

Fruit/creamy desserts
WHITE WINES: Riesling, Chenin Blanc, demi-sec (slightly sweet) Champagne, White Zinfandel

Raspberry, cherry/dark berry desserts
RED WINE: Merlot

Cherry pie
RED WINE: Syrah/Shiraz

Cheesecake
WHITE WINE: Chardonnay

Light cakes/baked apples
WHITE WINE: Riesling

Chocolate mousse
RED WINE: Syrah/Shiraz

Chocolate
WHITE WINE: late-harvest Riesling
RED WINE: the strong flavor of dark, bittersweet chocolate goes well with Cabernet Sauvignon.

HOME ENTERTAINING

Of course, all of these suggestions are valid for your home dinner parties too. If you plan on serving casual foods, here are some good wine choices:

Pizza, hamburgers, meat loaf
RED WINES: Zinfandel, Syrah/Shiraz, Merlot

Barbeque
RED WINES (fruity or spicy to go with charbroiled flavor): Zinfandel, Petite Syrah

None of the experts know about *chulent!* You may want to start with Pinot Noir, as it opens the taste buds, and then move on to a hearty red wine of your choice, maybe a Cab or a Merlot. If your *chulent* is really exotic, go off the deep end with a spicy Shiraz.

Tip!
If a guest brings a bottle that doesn't match the food of your dinner menu, serve it as an aperitif before the meal.

Wine and Cheese: A Perfect Match!

Paired for centuries, wine and cheese seem to be made for each other. There are no hard rules as to which wines should be served with particular cheeses, and the number of possibilities is staggering.

As in pairing any food with wine, my rule of thumb prevails here: your personal taste is the most important factor! If you prefer a particular cheese with a particular wine, nobody can say you're wrong.

But if you want to follow the accepted guidelines, think in terms of harmony: the cheese and the wine should have similar intensities (as in all food-wine pairings!). Powerful cheeses should be paired with strong wines, while delicate cheeses should be paired with lighter wines.

Over the years, these general pairing guidelines evolved:
- White wines match best with soft cheeses and milder flavors.
- Red wines match best with hard cheeses and stronger flavors.
- Fruity and sweet white wines and dessert wines work best with a wide range of cheeses.
- The more pungent the cheese you choose, the sweeter the wine should be.

More specifically:

Soft white cheeses. For mild cheese that is slightly sharp and salty, try out a sweet wine such as Riesling or Gewürztraminer. The more solid Bries need a full-bodied, fruity red like Pinot Noir or even a rich white, such as Chardonnay. Creamy cheeses go well with Champagne.

Fresh cheeses. For cottage or ricotta cheese dishes, use a fresh, light, crisp white wine like Sauvignon Blanc. Red wines are too heavy.

Semi-soft cheeses. These sliceable soft cheeses include Gouda, Monterey Jack, and Tilsit. Use full-bodied whites such as Gewürztraminer or Oaked Chardonnay, or light, fruity reds such as Red Zinfandel or Red Burgundy.

Semi-firm cheeses. The firmer, distinctively flavored cheeses such as Cheddar or Edam need wines such as Chianti or Merlot.

Hard cheeses. (Examples: Parmesan, Roquefort, some Swiss, Gruyère) These cheeses have a great range, from mild to strong and sharp, so most wines are a potential match. Remember, the stronger the cheese, the more full-bodied the wine. The mild ones will go nicely with something red and fruity, maybe Merlot, while the medium and stronger ones can be paired with Cabernet Sauvignon or Shiraz.

Tips on Accompaniments

- When serving cheese and wine, remember that pickles can overpower, and if you serve chutneys, they should not be spicy. Arugula, spring onions, olives, or celery can be served with cheese. Dried fruits such as figs, prunes, and raisins are delicious with all kinds of cheese.

- Biscuits and crackers tend to take away from the texture of the cheese and are often salty, so try fresh breads instead. Fresh rustic bread with a crisp crust is a perfect match for your wine and cheese.

ADVANCED CRITERIA FOR WINE SELECTION

IF YOU'VE PROGRESSED beyond the sniff-and-taste stage, you're likely to look for more sophisticated guidelines for selecting a wine (whether at a restaurant or at home). You have heard about rating codes and superior vintage years, and you're probably wondering what they mean. I'm not saying they should weigh heavily in your decision about a particular wine, but it's worth knowing about how they work.

Breaking the Rating Code

In recent years, the wine-rating system has become one of the wheels that keep the wine industry turning. It also has become a little overused, and for many wine consumers it may well be meaningless.

These ratings are the quick judgments that wine critics provide and are expressed numerically. Retailers and wine vendors use them to promote their wares. A wine with a higher rating is normally more expensive than average wines, although this is not always true.

To me, rating scales are useful if I'd like to try a new wine and want to avoid an unpleasant surprise. The problem is that wine scores are subjective. It all depends on the person doing the rating, and if I may say so, his or her mood on that day. It's always a good idea to go back and read the notes to see what produced the score, or find someone whose taste in wines runs parallel to your own and see what he or she thought about the wine

you'd like to try. Of course, this means you'll have to sample a few bottles to rate the raters before you find one with whom you agree.

One of the most respected wine-rating systems is the one developed in 1978 by the renowned wine critic Robert Parker when he started a wine-buying guide called *The Wine Advocate*. The scale was modeled after the American school grading system that goes from 50 to 100 points: it awards a set number of points for color, appearance, aroma and bouquet, flavor, and overall quality. In reality, Parker's scale really operates between 70 and 100 points. The wine always starts at 50 points and they all are given some points during evaluation. Wines rated over 80 are very good and over 90 are excellent.

The wines in the range of 90 and 95 are considered outstanding wines of exceptional complexity and character. In short, these are terrific wines. A wine scoring 96 to 100 is a really extraordinary wine possessing the highest levels of complexity and character, and displaying all the attributes expected of a classic wine of its variety. Wines of this caliber are worth a special effort to find. But their scores tend to be slightly murky, as the differences between them would be difficult to pin down. Parker himself once said that the only difference between wines in the 96 to 100 range is the emotion of the moment.

So how does the wine critic arrive at a score? During a wine-rating review, the wine tasters use an evaluation form called the "tasting sheet." The form is divided into sections. Each section represents a rating step grouped into categories: visual quality, nose quality, mouth quality, and overall quality.

- Visual quality evaluation examines the color properties of the wine and its appearance when viewed against light.

- Nose quality evaluation is an examination of the aroma complexity, its intensity, and how both relate to the *terroir* and the grape variety. The rating defines smell by aroma (floral, spicy, fruity, earthy) and intensity (powerful, medium, weak).

- Mouth quality evaluation measures the flavor, strength, balance, smoothness, and the sensation left in the mouth after the wine has been drunk. The rating defines tastes by flavors in the wine such as sugar (dry, sweet, very sweet), astringency (tannic, hard, closed), acidity (green, refreshing, balanced), body, and length (aftertaste – long, short).

- Overall quality evaluation examines the sensation produced by the wine as a whole and not as in the previous evaluation steps. The wine is evaluated on how typical it is of the region in which it was produced, its vintage, and aging.

As I stressed earlier, these ratings are not carved in stone and should not cause concern if you happen to like a low-rated wine or don't appreciate one with a high rating. Those scores are only somebody's opinion offered for your consideration.

What Year Is Best?

When I asked wine critic Daniel Rogov, *z"l*, about vintage reports, this is what he told me:

> The first formal vintage tables appeared in the 1820s and since then wine lovers have relied on them to help make their buying and drinking decisions. As popular as they are, however, it is important to remember that all vintage tables involve generalizations. These charts are meant to give an overall picture – and in making one's decisions it is wise to remember that the quality of wines of any vintage year in any region can vary enormously between wineries. Also worth keeping in mind is that vintage tables refer mostly to quality wines and not to simpler table wines, which are not intended for aging. Moreover, estimates are based on wines that have been shipped and stored under ideal conditions. We speak of drinking wines in terms of their maturity: wines are in their "youth," "adolescence," "early adulthood," or "maturity." What an individual prefers in this regard is very much a matter of personal taste.

Below are short reports on nine recent vintage years. (The chart describes only kosher wines and does not necessarily represent the quality of the overall harvest for non-kosher wines in each region.) Vintage years are rated on a scale of 20–100 and these numerical values can be interpreted as follows:

100 = Extraordinary

90 = Exceptional

80 = Excellent

70 = Very good

60 = Good but not exciting

50 = Average but with many faulted wines

40 = Mediocre/Not recommended

30 = Poor/Not recommended

20 = Truly bad/Not recommended

NYT = Not yet tasted

Worldwide Kosher Vintage Chart

	Israel	California	France Bordeaux	France Burgundy	Italy Piedmont	Italy Tuscany	Spain
2008	89	89	88	88	90	89	90
2007	89	90	86	88	90	86	86
2006	87	86	87	87	82	92	91
2005	90	90	94	92	92	91	90
2004	88	87	86	87	92	93	92
2003	89	90	90	88	86	90	86
2002	82	89	86	90	77	83	79
2001	90	91	90	86	91	91	85
2000	89	89	93	85	95	90	83

BACK TO THE RESTAURANT!

I LEFT YOU SITTING at your restaurant table, trying to figure out which wine to buy. So now that you know which wines would go best with your meal – and you may have taken the time to do your homework by looking up wine reviews, ratings, and vintage reports – you're ready to look that waiter straight in the eye. You've made your informed decision. The waiter smiles and goes off to fetch your wine. When he returns, the ritual of opening the bottle begins.

First, make sure that the bottle is still sealed. When he shows you the bottle, check the label to make sure it is actually what you ordered. Pay particular attention to the vintage date, if that was a consideration. If the vintage is different, ask for the correct bottle. If they don't have the bottle you ordered, make sure you are happy with the price and selection before you approve the bottle; otherwise, reorder.

After opening, examine the cork. The bottom of the cork should have coloration from the wine, but if there is wine on the body of the cork, it indicates that the cork may have shrunk during shipping and failed to protect the wine. The server will pour a small amount in your glass. Look at it. If the wine is clear, move on to swirling the wine in the glass. After the swirl comes the sniff. Take a good whiff of the wine. All you are looking for here is off odors. Watch out for smells like wet cardboard, vinegar, or rubber. None of these are good. If unsure, smell again or ask your server. If the smell is strong, send it back.

Now taste the wine. Chances are that if the wine has passed the first two tests, it is unlikely to taste bad. Once you have tasted the wine and feel it is not faulty, a simple nod or "It's fine" will inform the server to start filling the glasses. He will now decant the wine, if necessary, and then fill the guests' glasses first and finish with your glass.

In most fine dining establishments, the server will refill your glasses as needed. But if your glass runs empty, feel free to pour more yourself. It's your wine – you've earned it!

CHAPTER EIGHT

Storing Your Wine

Most wines are not made for long-term cellaring; in fact, the vast majority of wine is consumed within a short time after purchase. Winemakers know this and release many of their wines ready to be consumed immediately.

SO WHY BOTHER CELLARING? With time, the fruit, alcohol, tannin, and acid components in many wines will blend together and create a much better-tasting wine that is more balanced and more enjoyable. For a wine to get better with age in the cellar, it must have the right characteristics: flavor concentration, good acidity, tannin, and balance. Both red and white wines can have one or more of these characteristics, but generally red wines improve more from aging.

Let's get rid of the misconceptions. While the expression "wine cellar" brings up images of underground caves, it may be any space dedicated to storing wine. Differences between wine cellars are enormous. Vast caves storing thousands of bottles at unvarying temperatures are at one end of the scale, while a small cupboard is at the other end. Keep in mind that all wine cellars exist for the same purpose – to store wine in an ideal environment. Moreover, when most people think of cellaring wines, they tend to think of super-rare bottles that are too expensive for the average person. That's not completely true, but bear in mind that not all wines will improve dramatically through cellaring. A mediocre bottle will remain mediocre no matter how long you store it.

So we'll assume that you've found a wine that suits your taste. You feel the winemaker has brought out the best in his vineyard; you can taste the loving care that went into this wine and you have a hunch that it will taste even better with aging. Once that magic has been captured in a bottle, the ball is in your court. You should purchase at least a case of it. This way you can track its development and determine if it's still "closed," if it's "peaking," or if it is past its prime.

Whether or not your goal is to age the wine, if you are going to keep the wine for more than a month or two, it should be stored properly. The optimal storage option for wine in the long term is having it kept underground in a cellar built for that purpose: the temperature is cool (55°–60°F) at a constant 60 percent humidity. For many, that's an impractical and costly option. There are facilities that can store your wines, and some high-end wine retailers offer this service at a fee.

But let's say you want to cellar your wine at home. Bear in mind that wine has three enemies: light, heat, and lack of humidity. You can purchase a controlled-climate wine cooler and place it in a cool, dark room. If that is not an option, follow the Tips for Home Wine Storage.

Tips for Home Wine Storage

Keep it cool. Find a cool spot that is also dark, and is not too dry. It could be under the stairs or in a closet, as long as you aren't going to open or use it very often.

Avoid sunlight. Keep the bottles out of direct sunlight. Prolonged exposure to light can change the chemical structure of a wine. Wine bottles, especially for red wines, are made from dark glass for this reason. Yet dark glass alone is not enough to keep a wine in its original condition for very long.

Stay steady. Heat is probably worse for wine than light. Wine can easily start to taste cooked after just a few weeks at higher temperatures. To avoid this, find the coolest spot in your home (as close to a constant 55°–60°F as possible). An even more important consideration than the actual temperature is the constancy of it. When temperature rises and falls, it invariably causes the cork to expand and contract and let air into the wine bottle, which leads to oxidation.

Lay it down. Store bottles on their sides so that the corks stay in contact with the wine. If you let a wine bottle stand vertically too long, the cork will shrink enough to allow air into the bottle and oxidize the wine.

These are fairly simple rules. The idea is to protect your wine, and let it blossom into its full potential. When you're ready to break out one of those bottles – whether you're having friends over for dinner or celebrating a special occasion – there is great pleasure and satisfaction in being able to choose a wine from your collection, pulling out its cork and enjoying the benefits of proper storage and aging. Like a wise, elderly person, your wine has acquired depth from its experiences and it is ready to share its message. Treat it with respect.

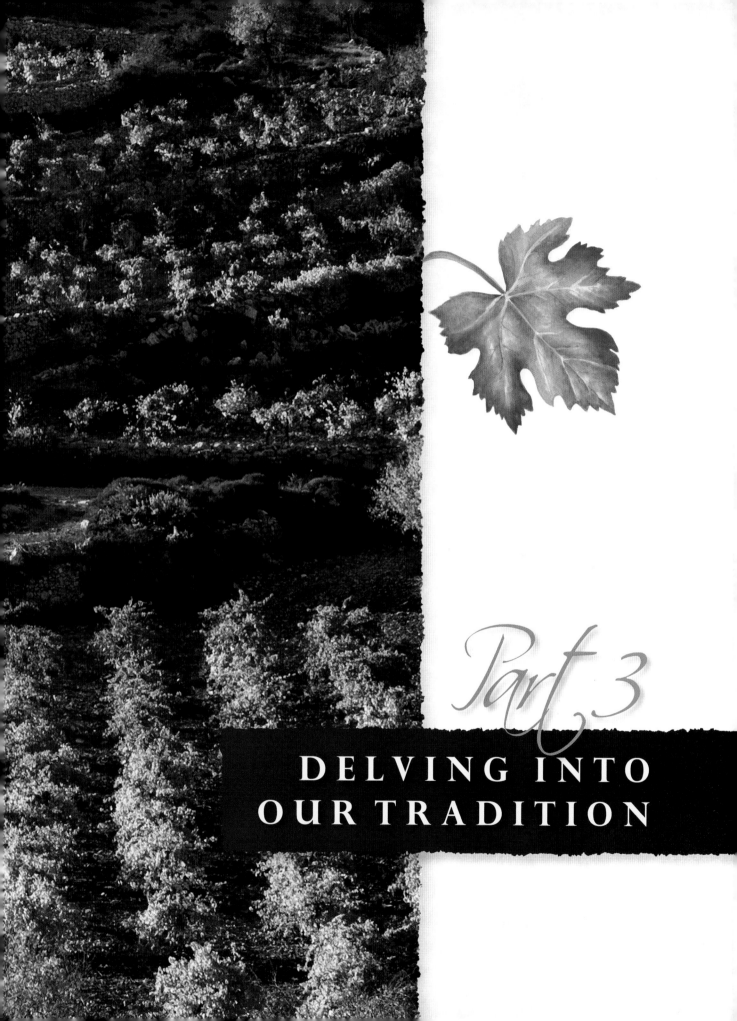

Part 3

DELVING INTO
OUR TRADITION

CHAPTER NINE

What Did the Sages Drink?

Remember that story in the Haggadah recounting a Passover Seder at which Rabbi Eliezer, Rabbi Yehoshua, Rabbi Elazar ben Azaryah, Rabbi Akiva, and Rabbi Tarfon were gathered? Imagine you were hosting this Seder; you would get the best of everything for these amazing guests! What kind of wine would they like? I'll bet you're thinking, "I'd get them the best Kiddush wine in town, thick and sweet!" Until recently, I would have done the same, because even as a great lover of dry red wines, whenever I would think of *Chazal* – our great sages of the Talmudic era – I imagined them sipping thick, syrupy, sweet wines. What else?

NOBODY EVER TAUGHT ME THIS; it's just something I believed. I suppose that is because most of us grew up with sweet wine served at sacred times – sweetness and tradition seem entwined. This is all the more true in my case because I grew up in a Polish Hungarian family. In that part of the world, food would be spiced with salt, pepper, sugar, and vinegar. Holiday and Shabbos delicacies were mostly sweet, and this helped make a positive connection between spirituality and sweetness. Deep in our guts we feel that sweetness is a "Jewish" thing.

This is not entirely wrong on one level. There happens to be a connection between the spiritual dimension and the quality of sweetness. Concerning the words of Torah, Psalms 19:11 declares, "They are sweeter than honey and drippings of the honeycomb!" Let me point out that the verse doesn't say that Torah is as sweet as honey; it says Torah is *sweeter* than honey. Honey is a material kind of sweetness, but Torah takes you beyond material sweetness to a form of joy that is so much more intense.

To my mind, this idea suggests a natural metaphor with a dry fine wine. You may find this unbelievable at first, but I promise you it is true. In a good wine, when the tannins are delicately balanced, and when your mind is ready and your taste buds are sensitized, the dry of the wine will surprise you with sweetness! The tannins come together with the tart tastes and the fruity impressions, and suddenly, the sweetness bursts out at you. To the best of my knowledge, sugar has nothing to do with this sweetness. Rather, it arises out of the interplay of the wine's other tastes. In my opinion, this sweetness is much more intense and delightful than the sweetness that comes from sugar and honey. To me, wine symbolizes how a person's life can grow from the material into the spiritual. A person moves from an ordinary experience of sweetness to a really sublime sweetness. Wine has helped me understand life beyond the physical, and that the greatest joys are those that can't be experienced in the material world.

SOME *HALACHOS* OF KIDDUSH

ONE DAY, I was learning the laws of Kiddush in the *Shulchan Aruch* (Code of Jewish Law), where I came across the following points:[1]

> 1. One should not make Kiddush over wine that has a bad smell, even if it both smells and tastes like wine. One should not make Kiddush over wine that has sat uncovered.
>
> 2. Wine from the press may be used for Kiddush; in addition, a person may squeeze out a bunch of grapes (into a cup) and recite Kiddush over it for the holy day.
>
> 3. One may recite Kiddush over wine taken from the mouth of a barrel, even if it has white particles, and on wine taken from the bottom of the barrel, even if it has sediment. Similarly, one may recite Kiddush over black wine, over sweet wine, and over wine that tastes like wine but smells like vinegar. *Nevertheless it is preferable to choose a good wine for Kiddush.*
>
> 4. One may make Kiddush over white wine. However, the Rambam disqualified it from Kiddush completely…and the custom is like the first opinion.
>
> 5. One may make Kiddush on cooked wine or wine that has honey in it. However, some say that one may not make Kiddush over them.

At first I couldn't believe my eyes! Point 3 is saying that sweet wine isn't good wine. It is in the category of wine with particles, wine with sediments, black wine, and wine that smells like vinegar! So I said to myself, "Maybe it is referring to wine that was sweetened with sugar, and that is why sweet wine is not preferred." Imagine my surprise when I discovered the even more extreme opinion cited in point 5: wine with a sweetener added is *so* inferior that you shouldn't make Kiddush on it altogether!

(Much to the relief of the makers of sweet kosher wine, most authorities, including the Rema, do not rule according to that opinion, and hold that a wine with added sweetener can be used for Kiddush!)

That really amazed me. Now we need to research what kinds of wine were available to our ancient sages, which ones were considered good, which were considered not-so-good, and what were the reasons for categorizing wines one way or another.

---

[1] The first four points that follow are from *Orach Chayim* 272:1–4. The fifth point is from 272:8.

Kiddush and the Altar

When people write on Jewish law they commonly introduce themselves by saying that they are merely proposing ideas for consideration, and that they are talking theoretically, not providing practical guidance. That is certainly true here. I am just a curious Jew with an interest in wine, sharing the fruits of my research.

With the help of Rabbi Spirn, I worked on two portions of Gemara: *Bava Basra* 97a–b and *Menachos* 86b–87a. In writing up our findings here, I am going to paraphrase the Gemara rather than quote it word for word. I am limiting myself to discussing passages that are relevant to the laws in the *Shulchan Aruch* that I quoted above.

Let us begin with the status of sweet wine

for Kiddush. (I don't mean "sweetened" wine, which seems to be a whole different issue and will be discussed later. I am referring to naturally sweet wine.) As I stated in the chapter "Charting Our Course," sweet wine can be made in a number of ways. Usually the winemaker exposes the grapes, while still on the vine, to some natural force that sucks the water out of the grape and concentrates the juice. The grapes may be shriveled by the sun, frozen by snow, or attacked by noble rot. With the water content of the grape reduced, the juice that remains will be highly sweet and concentrated. It remains sweet even after it has been fermented and turned into wine.

The first thing you need to know about the laws of Kiddush wine is that our use of wine is connected to the use of wine on the Altar that stood in the *Beis Hamikdash* in ancient Jerusalem. Wine was poured as an offering every day. At the moment the wine was poured, the Levites in the Temple would break into song. And Rav Achai Gaon wrote (in *Sheiltos* #54) that one of the reasons for making Kiddush on wine is that Kiddush is a form of "song." So there is a real connection between the holiness of the Altar and the recitation of Kiddush at the Shabbos table.

As in everything pertaining to the Temple service, there are clear criteria regarding what may be offered on the Altar. Certain kinds of wine are ideal. Others are less than ideal, but would be acceptable in times of emergency or duress (when the most suitable wines are not available). These kinds of wine would also be accepted *b'di'eved*, "after the fact" (if they were used by mistake). And some wines are so unsuitable that even in the worst of situations they may not be offered; they are simply *passul* (unfit) for the Altar.

The principle that Kiddush wine is connected to Altar wine is stated in the Talmudic tractate *Bava Basra* 97a: "Rav Zutra bar Tuviah said in the name of Rav: 'One may not recite the Kiddush of a holy day except on wine that is fit to be poured on the Altar.'" The Gemara goes on to qualify that statement: Wine does not have to be fit for the Altar *l'chatchilah* (a priori) in order to be kosher for Kiddush. If a wine is acceptable for the Altar, even *b'di'eved* (after the fact), then it may be used for Kiddush without hesitation. Only a wine that is *totally* unfit for the Altar – under all circumstances and even after the fact – may not be used for Kiddush at all. I call this the "Altar Rule." It will come into play later in our discussion.

Concerning the wines offered on the Altar, the Mishnah (*Menachos* 86b) spells out two *halachos*:

1. One should not bring "Heliston"; but if it was brought, it is kosher after the fact.

2. Sweet wine should not be brought…and if it was brought, it is completely unfit (*passul*).

Since Heliston was a kind of sweet wine (I'll explain this soon), the Gemara rightly sees a contradiction between these two laws: if Heliston is okay after the fact (or when nothing else is available), why are other sweet wines totally unacceptable?

Before we learn the Gemara's answer, let's define "Heliston." The name sounds like one of those Greek words that got absorbed into Hebrew. Since *helios* is the Greek word for sun, it struck me that Heliston might be "sun-wine," which would be wine made from grapes left to sweeten on the vine. And sure enough, when I looked further into the Gemara that is exactly what I found. Heliston refers to what we call today "late-harvest wine," namely wine made from grapes that were left out on the vine in the sun to shrivel, compressing their sweetness.

But what, then, is the "sweet wine" mentioned in the Mishnah? It seems to have been made out of a grape that nature endowed with extremely high sugar content. Was there really such a thing? Yes. I recently discovered that the Judean Hills indeed host a few obscure grape varieties with enough sugar content to yield a sweet wine without any special treatment or additives! Prior to this revelation, I had never heard of sweet wine being made just by fermenting grapes. Apparently this is possible if you start with super-sweet grape varieties, and such a variety was available in Judea in ancient times.

Let's get back to the contradiction. If Heliston is undesirable for the Altar, but acceptable after the fact, why are other sweet wines totally unacceptable? The Gemara gives two answers: One answer, put forth by Ravina, states that we are just not reading the Mishnah correctly. According to the true reading of the Mishnah, Heliston and sweet wine are in the same category and have the same law.

There are two ways to understand this. You can either assume that Heliston and sweet wine are both okay for the Altar after the fact (Tosafos), or you can take the opposite view and say that they are both absolutely unfit (Rashi). In my discussion here I will work with the view that according to Ravina both Heliston and sweet wine are acceptable after the fact (or when nothing better is available).

The second answer, given by Rav Ashi, assumes our original reading of the Mishnah to be correct. Rav Ashi answers the contradiction by asserting that there is a difference between Heliston and sweet wine. Here is what Rav Ashi says, and I find his words particularly intriguing: "The sweetness of the sun is not disgusting; the sweetness of the fruit is disgusting."

That is why Heliston is superior to regular sweet wine. When Rav Ashi refers to the "sweetness of the fruit," I suppose he is talking about that extra, over-the-top sweetness found in the original grape. Somehow this sweetness is "disgusting," rendering it totally

unfit for the Altar. In contrast, the sweetness caused by the grapes drying in the sun is not "disgusting." Heliston can be offered on the Altar when there is no alternative.

Two new questions have surfaced: What is the difference between these two kinds of sweetness? And why would one be "disgusting" while the other is fit for use?

Sun Sweetness and Fruit Sweetness

If my only purpose here were to demonstrate that *Chazal* thought that dry wine is superior for Temple and Kiddush use, I think I have proven my point. The simple fact that the sages quibbled over the acceptability of sweet wines means that they were not the most commonly drunk or highly regarded. But I am fascinated by that statement: "sweetness of the fruit is disgusting." That sounds very extreme to me. What is so bad about a little sweetness, some *zeeskeit* in your drink?

Let's revisit a point I made at the beginning of this chapter. I suggested that a dry wine – that is, a wine that has used up its sugar in the fermentation process – is like a person's soul going beyond the realm of physical pleasure to enter the realm of spiritual joy.

The whole point of the *Beis Hamikdash* and the Altar is to bring us to real spiritual life. Therefore only a fine dry wine would be offered up. Any amount of sugar left in the wine would symbolize a transformation that was incomplete. Imagine walking into Gan Eden with some material substance still stuck to you. It would be embarrassing, if not disgusting, in the pure light of Gan Eden. One might readily conclude that *any* sweetness disqualifies the wine from being used on the Altar.

Rav Ashi presents us with a major qualification of this idea. A grape that has more sugar than it can transform by fermentation (the sweet wine mentioned in the Mishnah) is seen as clinging to materiality. It is disgusting when viewed in the pure light of Gan Eden, which is entirely spiritual, and that's why it may never be offered on the Altar. However, a grape that was balanced and not overly sweet to begin with (like the Heliston mentioned in the Mishnah), and whose sweetness is the result of an outside force, does not have a negative kind of sweetness. One might say the grape was good and balanced, but it was a victim of circumstance.

So what about the view of Ravina that holds that all sweet wines are acceptable? How do we understand that? As the rabbis say, let me explain with a little parable. This one goes back at least a hundred years.

◀ Ancient winepress at Malkiya Vineyard, courtesy of Galil Mountain Winery

The Virtue of Mud

A wealthy man was being driven into town in his lavish coach on a rainy night. He came upon a poor man whose broken-down wagon was stuck in the mud; his old, skinny horse could not pull it free. Ordinarily the rich man wasn't the sort to offer help to strangers, but his compassion was aroused for the poor Jew shivering helplessly in the cold. He ordered his driver to hook up the old wagon to his horses, but even they couldn't pull the wagon out. The rich man was now committed to helping the poor man get on his way; seeing that there was no alternative, he stepped out of his fine warm carriage in his brocade garb and got down in the mud. The poor man, the rich man, the driver, and the horses all pulled together. Eventually, the pauper was on his way home.

Many years passed and the rich man died. Upon rising to the heavenly tribunal, his deeds were weighed; his good deeds went on one side of the scale, his bad deeds on the other. He had been greedy and selfish most of his life, and his good deeds were relatively few. They could not outweigh the burden of his bad deeds. A heavenly voice went forth, asking if there were any angels who knew of additional good deeds that could be put on the scale before the verdict was decreed.

One angel stepped forward. He recalled the rich man's kindness to the poor man that night; how he had saved his life, and by so doing also had saved the lives of his wife and children. The weight of those lives was placed on the scale – but the man's sins were still heavier. The angel noted that the rich man had actually gotten himself filthy and wet in the mud that night, something he had never done before. Shouldn't the mud count for something? A number of angels flew down to earth to bring up shovelfuls of mud. "Put it on the scale!" cried the heavenly tribunal. They threw the mud on the merit side of the scale, until slowly, slowly, it tilted downward. The rich man was saved.

To my mind, this story teaches two lessons, one obvious and one subtle. The plain message is never to turn down the chance to do a good deed. The subtle message is that when a Jew does a *mitzvah* he connects the physical to the spiritual, so that even the weight of the mud counts in heaven. It is transformed into a positive spiritual entity.

The tale can help us understand Ravina's opinion. Sugar may indeed represent materiality (as Rav Ashi holds), and since the Altar represents pure spirituality, really dry wine should be offered, because dry wine best represents the essence of spiritual life. However, in the real world there are many different kinds of people, and each has a special task. Some are meant to be constantly connected to spirituality, such as *Kohanim* in the *Beis Hamikdash* or great Torah sages. Some are meant to work with material things, to perform the commandments, and live an honest life. Yet all have a place in Gan Eden. G-d finds a way to transform the substance and material accomplishments of their lives into spiritual entities so they can gain entry into Gan Eden as well. And this could explain Ravina's opinion that a sweet wine could be acceptable on the Altar, at least in times of duress. If an individual has been true to his task in life, somehow G-d will accept that person's total experience in heaven. Sweet wine therefore does not necessarily conflict with what the Altar symbolizes, even if it fails to reflect the fullest extent of the Altar's deep spirituality.

The Altar Rule, Kiddush, and Naturally Sweet Wine

Remember the Altar Rule? Any wine that is totally unfit for the Altar is also unfit for Kiddush. According to Rav Ashi, naturally sweet wine (made from super-sweet grapes) is totally unfit for the Altar. And the Rambam rules in accordance with Rav Ashi (*Hilchos Issurei Mizbe'ach* 6:9). However, the conclusion of the *Shulchan Aruch* is that sweet wine *may* be used. (Recall point 3 from the *Shulchan Aruch* that I quoted above: "…one may recite Kiddush over black wine, *over sweet wine*, and over wine that tastes like wine but smells like vinegar.")[2]

<hr>

[2] Based on the Rambam just cited, the Chofetz Chaim concludes that sweet wine should not be kosher for Kiddush (*Biur Halachah* 272:3). In explanation of the ruling of the *Shulchan Aruch* see further in the text and the following footnote.

I think there's an easy way to understand the *Shulchan Aruch*: he rules like Ravina, that sweet wine (*all* sweet wine, whether dried by the sun [Heliston] *or* naturally sweet) is acceptable for the Altar after the fact. And according to the Altar Rule, such wine is acceptable for Kiddush![3]

Why then does the *Shulchan Aruch* conclude point 3 by saying that "it is preferable to choose a 'good' wine for Kiddush"? It seems to me that since sweet wine – and indeed, all the other types of wine mentioned in point 3 – are really not supposed to be used for the Altar (they're only acceptable after the fact, or when nothing else is available), it's preferable not to use them for Kiddush. This doesn't mean they're not completely acceptable, but it does mean that these are not the most *mehudar* (ideal) wines for the *mitzvah* of Kiddush; the ideal wines are those that may be used for the Altar even *l'chatchilah* (a priori).[4] Perhaps the *Shulchan Aruch* is teaching us that it is a special *mitzvah* to make the Shabbos table as similar to the Altar as possible!

<hr>

[3] In support of this thesis, I refer the reader to Tosafos in *Menachos* 87a, who says that the whole Gemara in *Bava Basra* 97a–b follows Ravina's opinion and not Rav Ashi's. (For a different approach to explain the ruling of *Shulchan Aruch* [and to respond to the argument of the *Biur Halachah* cited above], see Rav Wosner's responsa *Shevet HaLevy*, vol. 9, siman 58, based on the Meiri to *Pesachim* 108b.)

[4] This is a *chiddush*. However, it seems to me that it is correct, for the list in point 3 perfectly matches the list of wines mentioned in *Bava Basra* 97b that are only acceptable for the Altar after the fact (and which are therefore kosher for Kiddush because of the Altar Rule), and yet point 3 concludes that it is preferable to use a different wine. A careful comparison of the two lists also lends support to our thesis that the *Shulchan Aruch* rules like Ravina, because the *Shulchan Aruch* uses the word *masok* (sweet [wine]) in place of the Gemara's word *Heliston*. In other words, the two are halachically one and the same, as Ravina says!

THE "GOOD GRAPE"

WE HAVE LEARNED THAT according to Rav Ashi, a "super-sweet" grape, that is, a grape that is inherently so sweet that it can yield sweet wine without any special treatment or additives, is unsuitable for the Altar; however, if a grape only became super-sweet in the sun, it is suitable. I think we can derive a very helpful concept from Rav Ashi's opinion, and that is the concept of the "good grape." If a grape is properly balanced, so that it *could* complete fermentation with little or no sugar left over, it is a "good grape," and whatever comes out of it is acceptable for the Altar. This is true even if the grape became super-sweet in the sun, where circumstances prevented it from fulfilling its potential.

And, by the way, that is why grape juice that was squeezed right before Shabbos is acceptable for Kiddush even though it is inherently sweet, as stated in point 2 of the excerpt from the *Shulchan Aruch*: "a person may squeeze out a bunch of grapes [into a cup] and recite Kiddush over it for the holy day." The grape itself is "good" and is capable of using up its sugar if it were to go through fermentation. It follows from the Altar Rule that since, as the Gemara says (*Bava Basra* 97b), grape juice is acceptable for the Altar after the fact, it is acceptable for Kiddush without hesitation.

Ravina, on the other hand, holds that unusually sweet grapes (that can produce naturally sweet wine) are actually "good grapes" also. After all, these species of grapes

were *created* super-sweet. Just as we need to judge our fellow Jews favorably, we need to look at the overly sweet grape as having its own special path toward becoming wine. Certainly it didn't ask to be made super-sweet!

This concept of the "good grape" got me thinking. If there is such a thing as a "good grape," there must be something that is a "not-good grape." If Ravina considers the super-sweet grape "good," what would he consider "not-good"? One that is insufficiently sweet?

I found my answer in the Mishnah in *Menachos*. Among the things listed as being totally unfit for the Altar is "smoked wine." And what is that?

Smoke and Fumes

Nowadays there are certain wines that are said to possess a smoky flavor. They are called fume wines, and are made from the white Sauvignon Blanc grape. But these wines are not really smoked in any way, and they definitely are not what the Mishnah has in mind.

It occurred to me that there's another kind of smoked wine that comes from grapes that were exposed to smoke from forest fires. The smoke finds its way into the grapes, giving them a smoky taste, which then goes into the wine that is made from those grapes. Wouldn't that be a "not-good" grape? This smoky taste is definitely not desirable, and I could see why the Mishnah would not want this wine offered on the Altar. The taste has been altered by an undesirable outside influence.

Rashi offers an illuminating comment explaining what the Mishnah means by "smoked wine." (Recall that Rashi lived in Troyes, a central location in the famous Champagne district of France, and he himself was a vintner.) According to Rashi, smoked wines are made from bitter grapes that are "smoked" in order to sweeten them. Now, I don't know of any process today where grapes are exposed to smoke intentionally. Perhaps this was an old wine-making method for dealing with grapes that have too low a sugar content. But in any event, we have here a good example of a "not-good" grape: a grape that doesn't have enough sugar content to last through fermentation.

Clay Jugs, Particles, and Sediments

The concept of the "good grape" states that what comes from a good grape will be acceptable for the Altar. So let us go on with the Mishnah in *Menachos*: "One should not bring [wine for the Altar] from the mouth of the *chavis* [jug] because of the particles, or from the bottom because of the sediment, but rather one should draw it 'from a third of the way down or from its middle.'" At first I had no idea what this meant. Let's say that in the wine there was an upper level near the top of the jug where a layer of flour-like particles usually forms. How can you get past that layer to the clear wine underneath? Even if you pour carefully, the film will still get into your wine. Once again, thanks to Rashi, I got a crash course on wine-storing technologies in the ancient world.

First of all, we need to explain that the word *chavis* used in the Mishnah refers to the standard storage vessel used for wine in ancient times. It is not a barrel, as *chavis* is translated today. Back then, wine was stored and transported in earthenware jugs or containers. From studies of Roman history we know that containers called *amphorae* were used in the Talmudic era, and that these containers had narrow necks and pointy bottoms. (The narrow necks, I imagine, helped limit the amount of wine that would develop an upper layer of particles, while the pointy bottoms helped the sediment stay put once it settled.) The first Mishnah in *Pesachim* tells us that wine containers were stacked one on top of the other in the wine cellar.

Amphorae were generally stored on shelves with the pointy bottoms fitting snugly into large holes cut in the shelves. However, they also could be stacked by placing the pointed end of the upper amphorae into the space between the necks of the lower ones.[5]

The earthenware jug had an airtight seal fastening the lid. The lid was also made from clay, and wet clay was applied to bind the lid to the jug. That seal was pretty solid. For the most part, wine jugs were not opened by removing the lid, but rather by drilling a small hole in the side of the jug. A little tube was placed in the hole, forming a spigot, so the wine could flow into a decanter, or even into individual cups. Once the desired amount of wine was removed, the hole could be plugged with a stopper, or with a little more moist clay. So it was actually possible to take wine from a third of the way or halfway down the jug without disturbing the particles on the top or the sediment on the bottom.

Nowadays winemakers have a completely different way of dealing with particles, sediments, and other unpleasant things. A winemaker will simply add a clarifying agent, such as egg whites, to the barrel. This is a chemical concoction that bonds with all the particulates in the wine and settles them down at the bottom of the barrel over a ten-day period. One of the reasons kosher wine needs rabbinic supervision is to ensure that

[5] My thanks to Rabbi Leibel Reznick for this information. He mentioned also that in the Wohl Archaeological Museum (Herodian Quarter) in the Old City of Jerusalem there are six Jewish mansions from the Second Temple era. Some of the mansions have wine cellars stocked with Roman-style amphorae.

the clarifying agent is made from kosher ingredients. After the clarifying agent has done its work, the wine is gently pumped out, filtered, and bottled. (As you can see, in the

bottle. Although one might occasionally find a little more murkiness in an unfiltered wine, with some luck, the wine's natural texture will shine through.

Returning to the Mishnah in *Menachos*, we need to ask about the upper and lower layers of the wine where the particles or the sediment are located. Are these layers completely unfit for the Altar, or not desirable but acceptable after the fact? Interestingly, the Mishnah does not say, but the Gemara in *Bava Basra* 97b quotes a *baraisa* which states explicitly that the upper and lower levels in the jug are acceptable for the Altar after the fact. So here, I think, is another example of the "good grape" concept. If the grape is good, the wine that comes out of it is also acceptable, as long as it is the result of a natural process of development – even if it comes out in a form that is somewhat less than ideal.

How appropriate that sounds! As the Altar of Jerusalem is at the "center of the world," the wine that is *most* appropriate for it is the clear wine of the jug's center. But the murkier parts of the wine above and below the jug's center are basically acceptable, as well, since they are the natural products of a good grape.

time of *Chazal*, they dealt with the problem of particles and sediments in a more natural way!) For those who prefer a more natural texture to their wine, some winemakers bottle "unfiltered wine." There are some excellent unfiltered wines being made in Israel right now, which take great skill to

This idea of the wine from the center of the barrel being most fit for the Altar led me to think about the wine's color the same way.

Black, Red, and White

Color is not dealt with in the Mishnah in *Menachos* that we have been discussing. Rather we must turn again to the discussion in *Bava Basra* 97b. The Gemara there is trying to ascertain which wines can be used for Kiddush. It proceeds by applying the Altar Rule that "whatever is unfit for the Altar cannot be used for Kiddush, but whatever is acceptable for the Altar after the fact is suitable for Kiddush without hesitation."

It is a given that the ideal color of wine is red (see *Mishlei* 23:31, cited by the Gemara in *Bava Basra* 97b and *Pesachim* 108b). The Gemara asks: What about black wine and white (literally, "bright") wine? Are these precluded from being used for Kiddush by the Altar Rule? The Gemara replies, based on a *baraisa*, that since both these wines are acceptable for the Altar after the fact, they are indeed acceptable for Kiddush.

Here, too, I think it is interesting that the ideal color for wine is midway between the extremes of white and black. Since the Altar is in the center of the world, the wine most appropriate for it is bright red – not white, or black, or even deep purple. Nevertheless the entire range of colors is acceptable.

However, the opinion of the Ramban on this is noteworthy. He holds that the "bright" wine discussed in the Gemara is not completely white; it has at least a touch of redness in it (perhaps a blush or rosé). According to the Ramban, wines that are *completely* white are unfit for the Altar, and they are therefore disqualified from use for Kiddush as well. The

fact that some red color is essential for the Altar can be understood as follows: since the wine on the Altar symbolizes the transition between material and spiritual life, the wine's color has to be the color of life, which is red, for "blood is life" in the Scriptures. A clear white wine seems lifeless and fails to signify the vitality of spiritual life.

Although the *Shulchan Aruch* (272:4, quoted above) concludes that the custom is to permit making Kiddush on white wine, he does mention Ramban's strict opinion, which would seem to indicate that Ramban's opinion is an ideal. The *Mishnah Berurah* writes that the Ramban's opinion should be taken into account.[6] And common practice, from what I have seen, is indeed to prefer red wine for Kiddush.[7]

This color preference reflects a common theme in Jewish thought, articulated by the Rambam, that the *shvil hazahav*, the golden way, is the middle path. In the range of colors from white to black, red is the center, and this is what is identified as fitting for the Altar. This concept is also applied to the age of the wine. Wine that is kosher for the Altar is not too old (beginning to turn into vinegar) and not too young (unfermented grape juice); the central stage of the wine's life is the preferred one. Nevertheless, since both the young wine and the old wine come from "good grapes," they are still acceptable after the fact for the Altar.

---

[6] At least insofar as not using wines that are unusually white in color (unless nothing else is available). *See Mishnah Berurah* 272:12.

[7] I should note, however, that the Rema 472:11 says that if the white wine is of higher quality, it is better to use it.

THE ALTAR RULE: WHAT IS OUT?

WHAT KIND OF WINE, then, does the Altar Rule exclude from using for Kiddush? In the beginning of our discussion we learned that the Altar Rule does not disqualify any wine that is suitable for the Altar after the fact

or when no other wine is available So what did Rav have in mind when he formulated this rule?

The Gemara concludes that there are two kinds of wine disqualified for Kiddush use by the Altar Rule: (a) wine that has been left uncovered; and (b) bad-smelling wine.

Uncovered Wine

Let's talk about uncovered wine. Back in Talmudic times, it was understood that water or wine left uncovered might become contaminated by snakes, which would inject venom into liquids. One had to make sure that wine was kept covered at all times. Today, this concern does not exist in most places as snakes are not prevalent in areas of human habitation, so the *halachah* concedes that one need not worry about this.[8] But back then, wine that had been left uncovered and unguarded was potentially deadly. You hardly need the Altar Rule to tell you not to say Kiddush on it!

However, even in Talmudic times, the danger of snake venom could be eliminated by carefully straining the wine, and here the Altar Rule is applicable: uncovered wine, even if it has been strained, remains unfit for the Altar; and therefore it is unfit for Kiddush. It is dishonorable to use uncovered wine in an act of worship. This remains in force today, even when we are no longer concerned about the safety of uncovered wine.

Bad-Smelling Wine

"Bad-smelling wine" does not refer to wine that has a vinegary smell. That sort of wine is still acceptable for Kiddush as long as it retains the taste of wine. (The process of turning vinegary is also part of the life story of the good grape!) Nor do the words "bad-smelling wine" refer to any and all wines that you happen to feel have a less-than-pleasing aroma.

The Gemara defines "bad-smelling wine" as one that has picked up a bad smell from the vessel in which it was stored. This kind of smell would most likely originate from mold. In our day, a similar kind of bad smell would be the kind given to the wine by a bad cork. A wine like this is called "corked" wine, and it has the unpleasant scent of wet, mildew-infested cardboard. If you encounter a bottle of wine with this problem, absolutely do not use it for Kiddush! It is below standard quality.

The "exposed" wine and "bad-smelling" wine have substantial faults, which make their offering on the Altar an insult to G-d – similar to offering an animal with a physical blemish.

---

[8] Some people nevertheless are still careful today not to leave liquids uncovered, particularly overnight.

▲ Ancient winepress at Yiron Vineyard, courtesy of Galil Mountain Winery

THE ALTAR RULE: WHAT IS IN?

NOW GET READY for a surprise. We are going to discuss certain types of wine that would seem to be disqualified for Kiddush by the Altar Rule – but are not! Just to give you a hint: we will be modifying our understanding of the Altar Rule. So here goes!

Diluted and Improved

The Gemara (*Bava Basra* 97b) discusses the status of diluted wine. It states first that it is completely unfit for the Altar, and then it asks whether the Altar Rule disqualifies it for Kiddush.

Before I proceed, I should point out that in ancient times, wine was always drunk in a diluted state, the preferable dilution being one part wine to three parts water. Our ancestors always made Kiddush over diluted wine and considered straight wine to be nearly undrinkable. In fact, historical sources point out that the Roman wines were usually very strong. A fine wine called Falernia could actually catch fire! In later times, many Rishonim, followed by the *Shulchan Aruch* (204:5) and Rema (272:5), noted that our wines are not as strong as wines in the ancient world, and therefore dilution is usually no longer necessary.

In a few words, the Gemara dispels the notion that the Altar Rule disqualifies diluted wine for Kiddush: "Would you say that the Altar Rule precludes diluted wine [from being used for Kiddush? Quite the opposite!] Dilution improves it!" The Gemara is saying that even though diluted wine is completely unfit for the Altar, it is *not* excluded from Kiddush by the Altar Rule. How can this be?

What we see from this Gemara is that our understanding of the Altar Rule must be modified. The Altar Rule does *not* state simply that any wine that is not acceptable for the Altar is not acceptable for Kiddush. What it states is that any wine that is not acceptable for the Altar *because it is lacking in quality* is not acceptable for the Altar. That is to say, the Altar Rule is in reality a Quality Standards Rule. Uncovered wine and bad-smelling wine (discussed above) are not acceptable for the Altar *because they are lacking in quality*; that's why they are similarly not acceptable for Kiddush. Diluted wine is disqualified for the Altar – but *not* because it is lacking in quality.[9]

[9] The idea that the Altar Rule is in reality a Quality Standards Rule is developed by the *Aruch HaShulchan* 272:8–9.

We can get a handle on this matter by noting how undiluted wine is referred to throughout the Talmud: it is called *chai*, which means "raw." The Altar requires raw things in their natural state (Bechoros 17a).[10] No one would conceive of cooking sacrificial meat before putting it on the Altar. The wine offerings parallel the meat offerings; they too must be raw. Now certainly, for human consumption, cooked food is better than raw food, even though only raw food may be offered on the Altar. Similarly, even though diluted wine is an improvement over undiluted wine for our consumption, it is completely unfit for the Altar. Still I find it puzzling: how is it that wine fit for human consumption is "too good" for the Altar while it is fine for our Kiddush?

To put this question into perspective, I would like to suggest the following: As I have suggested earlier, the Altar symbolizes the transformation of physical life into spiritual life. But it functions on a scale that is totally beyond human experience. Its fire is a giant, consuming presence, burning with a force and fury that is both natural and supernatural. And that's why raw and undiluted power is the only way to go. Cooked or diluted materials are not right for a scale of such magnitude; they are inferior and unacceptable for the Altar.

But Kiddush is a different story. Although the Altar and the Shabbos table do correspond to each other (see above, "Kiddush and the Altar"), the Shabbos table is a scaled-down, human phenomenon. When it comes to Kiddush, dilution is an improvement because it reduces the wine's intensity so it can be consumed comfortably by human beings. Dilution makes the wine superior for our use. The fact that this wine is no longer suitable for the spirituality of the Altar is hardly a reason to disqualify it for Kiddush.

Clearly, a process that begins with a good wine from a good grape and makes it palatable to human tastes is a positive move, as we shall see as well in the coming segment.

Cooked Wine

Cooked wine is not mentioned in the discussion in *Bava Basra* about the Altar Rule. At first glance, it seems that cooked wine should be completely disqualified for Kiddush since, as the Mishnah in *Menachos* says, it is totally unfit for the Altar. Why didn't the Gemara mention it, along with exposed wine and bad-smelling wine?

Perhaps one could argue that once wine with a bad smell is disqualified there is no need to mention cooked wine separately, since it too has been degraded and its quality diminished by something outside its natural process. This, of course, assumes that cooked wine is qualitatively diminished. According to some of the Geonim, cooked wine is so diminished that it doesn't even qualify for the blessing of *borei pri hagafen*.[11] According to this opinion, it is quite clear that the Gemara doesn't bother disqualifying cooked wine because it isn't really regarded as wine! The

---

[10] See *Sifrei* to Bamidbar 28:7, where the sages derive that wine, specifically, must be *chai*.

[11] Quoted in the *Maggid Mishneh* on the Rambam, *Hilchos Shabbos* 29:14.

Rambam takes a less dramatic position than these Geonim, and writes that while cooked wine is indeed disqualified for Kiddush, it is still considered wine and retains the blessing of *borei pri hagafen*. According to the Rambam, cooked wine is disqualified for Kiddush by the Altar Rule – it fails the Quality Standards test.[12]

However, one can argue the opposite approach as well. If the Gemara has not disqualified cooked wine, perhaps we can assume that it *is* acceptable for Kiddush. But how would this assumption jive with the Altar Rule, given that cooked wine is disqualified from use on the Altar? We are compelled to say that, like dilution (discussed in the preceding section), cooking is actually an improvement to wine, at least from the point of view of human tastes and sensibilities.[13] Indeed, this is the opinion of many Rishonim.[14] Cooked wine therefore passes the Quality Standards test (the Altar Rule) and is acceptable for Kiddush.

This position sounds surprising to today's wine appreciators, for cooking seems to worsen the taste of a wine. Even the modern process of flash pasteurization, currently used to give some wines their *mevushal* status, is regarded as damaging to the wine's quality in at least a subtle way. But it seems that the perceptions of some of the ancient sages differed from ours: they considered the "wildness" of uncooked wine as somehow too overwhelming for human sensibilities. In that light, cooking could be seen as an adaptation of the wine's power to human proportions, rather than a degradation of its real essence.

What does the *Shulchan Aruch* say regarding the actual *halachah*? As quoted above (point 5), "*one may make Kiddush on cooked wine* or wine that has honey in it. *However, some say that one may not make Kiddush over them.*" It seems that the *Shulchan Aruch* recommends against using cooked wine for Kiddush. The Rema writes that Ashkenazic custom is to use cooked wine for Kiddush – but only if it is superior to the other available wines.[15]

The Debate over Sweetened Wine

We are now ready to tackle the status of sweetened wine,[16] a subject of debate between the Rambam and most other authorities. The Torah (Numbers 2:11) says that no "honey" may be added to anything that goes on the Altar. "Honey" here is a general term covering all kinds of plant-derived sugars.[17] Even a drop of sugar added to a barrel of wine disqualifies that wine from going up on the Altar.

According to the Rambam, the Torah is telling us that sweeteners diminish the quality

---

[12] See preceding section, "Diluted and Improved."

[13] See *Mishnah Terumos* 11:1.

[14] As cited in the Beis Yosef, *Orach Chayim* 272:8.

[15] For as the *Mishnah Berurah* (272:23) explains, if equally good wine is available that is not cooked, it is proper to seek to fulfill the minority view cited in *Shulchan Aruch* (the view of the "some say") that one may not use cooked wine for Kiddush.

[16] That is, wine that has been sweetened with additives. This is a different discussion from the ones earlier in the chapter about "sweet wine," which dealt with wine that was sweet on its own – either because the grape had an unusually high sugar content (the "super-sweet" grape) or because the grape had been left in the sun (Heliston).

[17] See *Mishneh LaMelech, Hilchos Issurei Mizbe'ach* 5:1 and *Yabia Omer*, vol. 4, *Yoreh De'ah* 2:4.

of wine. Based on the Altar Rule (the Quality Standards Rule), the Rambam (*Hilchos Shabbos* 29:14) rules that if even a minute amount of sweetener was added to a wine, it may not be used for Kiddush. However, the Rosh and most other Rishonim disagree. According to the Rosh (*Bava Basra* 97b), sweetening a wine is another way of improving it and adapting it for human tastes. As proof, he notes that Konditon wine (which is made by adding sweetener and spices to regular wine) was considered by the Talmud Yerushalmi (*Pesachim* 10:1) to be acceptable for Kiddush!

We have noted in our introduction that sweet Kiddush wines were made originally because it was hard to get a drinkable wine out of the bitter Concord grapes available to kosher winemakers at the time. Those early winemakers were relying on the lenient opinion of the Rosh and similarly minded Rishonim.

Before we get to the *Shulchan Aruch*, a little Jewish philosophy: We have already encountered the notion that sweetness carries some negative connotations. The Torah doesn't say explicitly why honey must not be brought up on the Altar, but the *Sefer Hachinuch* (*mitzvah* 117) suggests that the Torah is trying to teach us some important lessons. First, don't get too wrapped up in sweets. Healthy food is the way to go! Second, some foods might represent a way of life that seeks pleasure for its own sake. Seeking spirituality, not hedonism, is the Jewish lifestyle. And the third message is about character development: honey represents arrogance. When we bring an offering to the *Beis Hamikdash*, we are supposed to develop the all-important trait of humility. Ramban (on Numbers 23:17) adds that honey, being ultra-sweet, is banned from the Altar because it lacks "balance" (a Kabbalistic idea that I, for one, would not pretend to understand!).

What does the *Shulchan Aruch* say about sweetened wine? As quoted above (at the end of the section "Cooked Wine"), the *Shulchan Aruch* seems to recommend not using sweetened wine for Kiddush.[18] And once again, the Rema writes that according

[18] See footnotes 15 and 16. The *Mishnah Berurah* cited there says the same about sweetened wine.

to Ashkenazic custom, sweetened wine is fine for Kiddush – but only if it is superior to the other available wines. I think the Rema is telling us that sweetening, like cooking, is acceptable only if and when it can be viewed as an improvement. However, to a person who possesses a fine uncooked or unsweetened wine, cooking and sweetening will not seem like improvements. To that person, these actions will cause unnecessary alterations to the wine – and diminish its quality.

It follows from our discussion that there is no reason to favor sweet wines for Kiddush. Wine that has been artificially sweetened is not the preferred choice of either the *Shulchan Aruch* or the Rema. And wine that is naturally sweet, we have learned, is not ideal either![19]

So is it possible to have a sweet wine that meets the ideal standards of Jewish law?

Kosher winemakers have come up with a way. Sweet wines can be made by an inexpensive process called fortification.[20] This means that before the wine is completely fermented and there is still some sugar in the brew, some wine alcohol (such as brandy) is added. This kills all the yeast and leaves a sweet wine. Sometimes grape sugar is added as well, which is considered not to be an outside kind of sweetener, and is unproblematic. So you can make Kiddush over sweet wine with the full approval of the *Shulchan Aruch*!

[19] We have learned that grapes naturally make dry wine, with the exception of the super-sweet grapes discussed above. But besides being quite rare, we have seen (at the end of our discussion in "The Altar Rule, Kiddush and Naturally Sweet Wine") that they are still not ideal. The other way we learned one can produce naturally sweet wine is to use sun-dried grapes to make Heliston – but that would be very expensive; and according to what we wrote in footnote 7, Heliston is also not ideal!

[20] This was mentioned in chapter 3, "Charting Our Course," but I'll review it here.

SO WHAT DID *CHAZAL* DRINK?

I THINK IT IS PRETTY CLEAR that when a Jew said the word *yayin* (wine) in ancient times, the plain meaning of the word was dry red wine. There is a very simple reason for this. Unless you do something out of the ordinary to the grapes, or unless you start with unusually sweet grapes, you will get dry wine. Other kinds of wine need to be specified by name, e.g., sweet wine (made from super-sweet grapes), Heliston (made from sun-dried grapes), bright wine (made from white grapes), or Konditon (made by adding sweetener and spices to regular wine). Remember that Heliston and Konditon are not Hebrew terms, so I think it safe to assume that these wine-making methods were imported from the Greco-Roman world! The fact that the Talmud Yerushalmi needed to ask whether Konditon is suitable for Kiddush (and concluded that it is acceptable) means that it was not commonly used, at least not at first. I think it possible to infer that while the Greco-Roman world prized sugary sweet wines, traditional Jewish wine was dry and unquestionably suitable for offering on the Altar.

Based on all of these considerations, my conclusion stands: dry red wines are the true wines of the Land of Israel, and *Chazal* – our sages of blessed memory – drank dry!

Appendix 1
LINGO

A GLOSSARY OF WINE TERMS

aeration. Exposing wine to the air to let it absorb oxygen. Decanting the wine or swirling it in the glass are two common ways of doing this. Oxygen will allow the wine to release its aromas and tastes.

aftertaste. The flavor sensation provided by the wine after swallowing. Frequently referred to as the "finish" of a wine. Good wines will have complex and deep aftertaste.

age worthy. Only a small number of top wines have adequate character to undergo aging. A wine that is capable of being aged is referred to as age worthy. The majority of wines are meant to be enjoyed within several years of their release time.

alcohol. The intoxicating element of wine. It is produced by yeast during fermentation, as it eats up the sugar in the grapes.

American oak. A wood commonly used for making barrels for aging wine. It gives an intense flavor.

anthocyanins. The red stuff that gives wine its color.

aperitif. Wine taken before a meal.

appellation. A clearly defined area or region where the grapes were grown, such as Bordeaux, Alsace, Napa Valley, or Sonoma Valley. Many wines are esteemed because they come from particular places, and it is believed that location (a concept that includes soil type, weather, and amount of sunshine per year – see *terroir*) determines the ultimate quality of the wine. The French are particularly obsessive about location. Many wine names are actually place names. Today some areas of Israel are becoming valued as places where great grapes grow, so there are wines that carry an appellation such as "Mount Carmel Zinfandel."

Appellation d'Origine Contrôlée (AOC or AC). The hyper-complicated French system of appellations that ensures that only a vineyard growing within two hundred meters of the most outlying cowshed of the village of Vouvray may call its wine a "Vouvray." In order to get a certification under an appellation in this system, a wine must follow strict rules about the region in which the grapes were grown, the varieties used, the ripeness at harvest, and the techniques used in the growing and wine making.

aromatic wine. Wine to which herbs have been added, usually used in aperitifs. Vermouth is an aromatic wine.

balance. The harmony of the wine's characteristics and elements.

blush. Also referred to as "rosé." This term describes a pinkish-colored wine made from red grapes. The grape juice is not permitted to sit on the grape skins long enough to pick up all the red pigment. Some blush-colored wines are made simply by mixing reds and whites together.

body. The texture of a wine. A wine may be said to be light-bodied or full-bodied.

bouquet. The complexity of aromas that develops in fine wines. A wine can develop a truly amazing array of aromas. Detecting them is part of the joy of wine tasting.

brut. A French word used to refer to dryness, most often in sparkling wine.

buttery. A taste somewhat like the oiliness and flavor of melted butter. Many aged Chardonnays develop this flavor, which is considered a good taste.

capsule. The metal or plastic protective film that surrounds the top of the bottle. It is usually removed before pulling out the cork. You can be stubborn, if you like, and pull the cork out without cutting away the capsule, but then you will be left with jagged edges at the top of the bottle, and you may dribble wine as you pour.

chewy. Full-bodied, strongly tannic wines that are rich in texture may be referred to as chewy.

clean. An honest, straight wine with simple flavors.

coarse. A wine that is rough or harsh with too many tannins or woody tastes.

complexity. The coming together of the aromas, flavors, and richness of a fine wine.

corked, corky. A wine with a moldy smell caused by a defective cork.

crisp. The characteristic of elevated acidity, which makes a white wine refreshing and bright.

decanting. To pour a bottle of wine out into a special bottle with a big bulbous bottom. Doing this exposes most of the wine's surface area to oxygen and helps open up the wine's aromas and flavors.

Denominazione d'Origine Controllata (DOC). The Italians' attempt to out-French the French by creating a super-rigid system of wine regions and wine names. The Denominazione d'Origine Controllata Garantita (DOCG) has even tougher requirements.

earthy. A smell suggestive of soil and earth. In small amounts, it is appealing. Too much, and you feel like you're sipping mud.

***Eiswein* or icewine.** Wine made from grapes that were left on the vines until frozen by the first frosts of winter. This concentrates the grape juice and makes it very sweet. The yeasts can't eat up all the sugar before the rising alcohol level kills them. The wine remains sweet. *Eiswein* is an official German classification. Similar wines from other countries are called icewines.

elegant. Wines that are balanced and refined in character.

estate bottled. This means that the winemaker is in control of the vineyards and oversees their cultivation.

fermentation. The process in which yeast eats sugars and produces alcohol and carbon dioxide, thereby transforming grape juice into wine.

finish. The aftertaste wine leaves after swallowing. A longer finish is associated with better wine.

flat. Wine that lacks acidity. It is usually dull and unbalanced.

fleshy. A sensation on the palate that reminds the drinker of the fleshy character of plums.

flinty. A dry, mineral flavor that comes from limestone chips in the soil. This taste is often associated with wines such as Sauvignon Blanc.

flowery. Having the smell and taste of flowers. This is often a characteristic of white wines.

fortification or **fortified wine.** Adding alcohol (usually a grape brandy) to a fermenting wine, resulting in a sweet wine with high alcohol content (14–23 percent). This is an easy way of making a wine sweet without adding sugar. Many Sephardic Jews follow the opinion of the Rambam which holds that Kiddush may not be recited over a wine to which sugar has been added. Many sweet Kiddush wines made in Israel have been fortified with wine brandy, so they are both sweet and acceptable for Kiddush according to all the opinions. Port, Sherry Madeira, and Malaga are fortified wines.

foxy. An unpleasant musky taste in wines made from American grapes. Unfortunately, back in the old days this was the only kind of grapes kosher winemakers could obtain. They added lots of sugar or corn syrup to cover up the foxy quality. Even today, many people associate the word *kosher* with syrupy sweetened Concord grape concoctions.

grand cru. This means "great growing region" in French. This is an official appellation indicating the highest level of wine making.

harmonious. When all the wine's characteristics are perfectly balanced.

herbaceous. A wine that contains aromas reminiscent of herbs or spices. It is often found in Sauvignon Blanc and Merlot wines.

Indicazione Geografica Tipica (IGT). An Italian quality classification. A wine with this classification may be very good, but still not eligible to be included in DOC or DOCG standards.

intricate. Interweaving of subtle complexities of aroma and flavor.

late-harvest. A term indicating that a wine was made from grapes picked late in the season. These grapes have been left to shrivel on the vine so their juice is more concentrated, and the wine ends up being sweet.

legs. The viscous droplets that run down the side of the glass after swirling it. Pronounced legs are indicators of higher levels of alcohol content.

length. The length of time that a taste persists after swallowing. Fine wines should have a long finish, or aftertaste.

lively. Wines with characteristics of freshness, crispness, fruitiness, and some acidity.

luscious. Rich, opulent, and smooth; most often said of sweet wines but also intensely fruity ones.

magnum. A large-format bottle that holds 1.5 liters (as opposed to the standard 750 mililiters).

mature. Fully developed, ready to drink.

meaty. Full-bodied, concentrated, and chewy.

musty. Describing wine with stale, moldy, or mildew smell.

New World. Refers to countries that started wine production in recent history, including the United States, Australia, Argentina, New Zealand, Chile, and South Africa.

noble. The classic grape varieties that are used to produce the world's finest wines. Cabernet Sauvignon, Syrah, Merlot, Pinot Noir, Chardonnay, Sauvignon Blanc, Semillon, and

Riesling are some of the best-known "noble" grapes.

nose. The smell of the wine. Also called aroma or bouquet.

nutty. Describes nutlike aromas that develop in certain wines.

oaky. The aroma and flavor imparted from aging wine in oak barrels. It is characterized by smokiness, vanilla, clove, or other spices. Should be balanced and not overly pronounced.

off-dry. Not quite dry; indicates a slightly sweet wine.

old vine. This refers to wines made from grapes grown on vines over forty years old. Usually smaller yielding vines, they make more concentrated fruit which produce more complex wines.

organic wine. Usually refers to wines produced from grapes grown without the use of synthesized fertilizers, herbicides, or pesticides. Sulfur is still used in the fermentation process, but in minimal amounts.

oxidized. Lacking freshness, flat or stale in aroma and flavor. On the one hand you must expose the wine to oxygen so it will release its aromas and flavors. On the other hand, once you do that the oxygen will rather quickly deaden all the wonderful aromas and flavors it released (the precise amount of time this takes depends on variable factors such as whether the cork

is porous, whether the wine was stored in an oak barrel, and whether the glass is swirled after pouring). This is a major conundrum for wine drinkers. One solution is use a vacuum bottle sealer. You decant what you want for that sitting, and vacuum seal the rest. Some have found that refrigerating slows down oxidation, though afterwards you have to let the wine warm up in the decanter or glass and it will take longer than usual to open up. Perhaps the best solution is to share your wine with your friends so there are no leftovers to oxidize.

palate. The sense of taste, and specifically the areas of the mouth that process taste, smell, and texture of a wine in the drinker's mouth. Terms like *front palate*, *middle palate*, and *back palate* refer to where in the mouth a particular texture or flavor is expressed.

pip. Another term for grape seeds.

private reserve. Winemakers' term for their top batch of wine, often produced from selected vineyards.

robust. Full-bodied, powerful, heady.

rough. Biting, unpleasant taste associated with elevated levels of tannins.

rosé. French for "pink wine." See **blush**.

round. Smooth and well-developed flavor, without rough edges.

silky. A smooth, sinuous texture and finish.

smoky. Aroma and flavor sometimes associated with oak aging in charred barrels.

sour. Acidic or vinegary.

spicy. Having the flavors of mint, clove, cinnamon, anise, or pepper.

structure. The way wine holds together. A good wine must successfully integrate components such as acidity, tannin level, alcohol content, and other characteristics.

sulfur or **sulfites.** An anti-oxidant used in the wine-making process. As a result of fermentation, sulfite compounds occur naturally. People with asthma or allergies may have a reaction to this compound. Virtually all wines that are not organic are mandated to have warning labels with the phrase "contains sulfites." Sweet wines have the highest sulfite content, followed by white wines and lastly by reds, which have the lowest levels of sulfites.

sweet. The level of sugar content in wine. Generally indicates the presence of residual sugar that was not converted to alcohol. Sometimes sugar may be added to an inferior wine to mask other less desirable characteristics.

tannins. Natural components of the grape found to varying degrees in the skins, seeds, and stems of grapes. Tannin is mostly prominent in red wines. It acts as a natural preservative and helps wine age. It creates a dry, puckering sensation in young red wines and mellows with aging.

tartaric acid. The principal acid in grapes and wine; contributes to taste and stabilizes color.

terroir. A French term describing the interplay of soil, climate, topography, and grape variety in a specific site, which makes the wine from each site distinct. The French already stress the geographical location of the vineyards in their appellation system. However, wine appreciators who study *terroir* will note differences between one vineyard and the next even within a single area, and claim that each vineyard makes its unique qualities felt in its wine. Believers in the importance of *terroir* will prefer "single vineyard" wines, in which a single variety of grape from a single vineyard is used exclusively without blending or admixing. A single vineyard wine will give the greatest possible emphasis on the *terroir* of the vineyard and will generally have a strong single-minded quality about it. In France, the Burgundy region is most often associated with this wine-making method.

vanilla. A scent imparted by aging in oak.

varietal. A wine made from a single grape variety.

velvety. Smooth and rich in texture.

vin de pays. Country wine. This is one of the French quality classifications, indicating a wine produced in less prestigious regions that do not meet the restrictive Appellation Controlée requirements.

viticulture. The science or study of making wine.

yeast. The microorganisms that convert sugar to alcohol and carbon dioxide during fermentation.

HEBREW/ENGLISH GLOSSARY

Most words are Hebrew or Aramaic. When a word is Yiddish, it is noted in parentheses.

Admor. A Chassidic Rebbe. *Admor* is a Hebrew acronym which stands for "Our master, teacher, and rabbi." An *Admor* may stand at the head of a Chassidic *kashrus* supervising authority.

alter heim (Yiddish). The "old home" environment of prewar Europe.

Badatz. A Hebrew acronym that stands for *beis din tzedek*, "religious court of justice." Such courts represent the highest authority within the Orthodox communities and perform some supervisory functions not usually associated with courts of law, including overseeing the kosher supervision of food and beverage products.

baraisa. A teaching from the sages of the Talmud that was not included in the Mishnah.

Beis Hamikdash. The Holy Temple of Jerusalem which stood in ancient times. The first Holy Temple was destroyed by the Babylonians c. 586 BCE. The second Holy Temple was destroyed by the Romans c. 70 CE.

brachah. A blessing. Wine is considered very special in Judaism, and a unique blessing is recited ending in *borei pri hagafen*, "Who creates the fruit of the vine." After drinking wine, one may be obligated to recite an abridged version of the Grace after Meals called Me'ein Shalosh.

chavrusa. Torah study partner.

Chazal. Jewish sages of ancient times.

chiddush. A new insight into Jewish law or literature.

chulent. A Sabbath stew made most often with meat, beans, barley, and potatoes. There are numerous variations in recipes.

derech. Way of life.

drashah. An instructive elaboration on a Torah theme, often departing from its plain meaning.

Eretz Yisrael. The Land of Israel.

Gan Eden. Paradise.

Gemara. Talmud; the Oral Law of the Torah (which explains the Written Law of the Five Books of Moses).

Geonim. Post-Talmudic sages who lived c. 500–1000 CE.

golem. A robot-like individual.

Haftorah. A passage from a book of the Prophets read aloud in the synagogue.

halachah (pl. *halachos*). Jewish law. *Halachah* governs all areas of Jewish life, including dietary practices.

hamotzi. Name of the blessing said over bread.

Hashem. G-d. (Literally, "the Name.")

hechsher or **kosher symbol.** A symbol printed on the wrapper or bottle which indicates that the product inside has been produced under *kashrus* supervision. In America, such symbols include the "OU," the "Circle K," the "Star K," and many others. The symbols are usually unobtrusive and unnoticed except by the kosher consumer. The Israeli chief rabbinate does not usually use a symbol, but instead allows the words "Certified by the chief rabbinate" to be printed somewhere on the packaging. Badatz symbols tend to be more ornate and recognizable.

kashrus. The system defining the status of being kosher (fit for consumption by Jews according to Jewish law).

kashrus supervising authority. A group of rabbis and their assistants who supervise the production of kosher foods and drinks. Jewish consumers rely upon these authorities to certify that foods and drinks are kosher. The Israeli chief rabbinate and local municipal rabbinates often provide the bulk of such supervision in Israel. Badatz representatives sometimes add their supervision to products as well. See also **Badatz.**

kerem reva'i. Grapes grown during the fourth year counting from the planting of the vine. These grapes are holy and cannot be eaten unless they are ritually "redeemed" first. According to most authorities, *Kerem Reva'i* does not apply outside the Land of Israel. See also *orlah.*

Kiddush. Sabbath and holiday blessing over wine.

kilei hakerem. Forbidden vegetable-vine combinations. According to Torah law, a farmer may not plant any vegetable in a vineyard; the resulting grapes may become forbidden and non-kosher. Similarly, if a vegetable begins to grow on its own within a vineyard, the farmer must uproot it immediately.

Kohanim. Priests of the Holy Temple in Jerusalem, and their descendants.

Kosel Hama'aravi. The Western Wall (near the Temple Mount) in Jerusalem. This is the remains of a wall that surrounded the Holy Temple.

kosher. Fit for consumption by Jews according to Jewish law.

kos shel brachah. "Cup of blessing." This refers to the cup of wine held during the recitation of ritual prayers such as Kiddush.

matzo. Flat unleavened "bread" (more like a cracker) eaten particularly on Passover.

mesorah. Heritage; specifically the handing down of Torah tradition from generation to generation.

mevushal. "Cooked" or heated wine. Jewish law mandates that wine must be *mevushal* to be consumed when Jews and gentiles are in mixed company. This is an important concept in maintaining the kosher status of a wine, as only *mevushal* wines may be handled by non-Jews.

Midrash. A segment of Oral Law containing rabbinic lessons or lore.

Mishnah. The Oral Law, edited into final form

by Yehudah HaNasi in the second century CE.

mitzvah (pl. *mitzvos*). A Torah commandment (regarded as both an obligation and a privilege).

nazir. In Jewish law, one who commits himself to abstention from wine (as well as several other practices) as a spiritual discipline, usually for a specific period of time. This practice is no longer undertaken today. It is interesting to note that after the term of *nezirus* (being a *nazir*) was completed, a former *nazir* was required to bring a sacrifice in atonement for having forgone the permitted pleasure of wine.

orlah. Immature fruit. According to Torah law, any fruit that grows on a tree or vine is totally forbidden within the first three years after planting and no benefit may be derived from it. In the case of a vineyard, the first three years' produce are forbidden as *orlah*. The fourth year's produce is holy and must be eaten in Jerusalem or be ritually redeemed. Today, in the absence of the Holy Temple, we are not permitted to eat holy fruit, so one must redeem it. It is a responsibility of the supervising authority to ensure that no *orlah* or unredeemed fourth-year grapes are used in kosher wine. The laws of *orlah* apply both in the Land of Israel and outside of it.

Pesach. The Jewish holiday of Passover.

Rebbe (Yiddish). The spiritual leader of a Chassidic group.

Rishonim. Talmudic scholars of the Middle Ages.

Sanhedrin. The Jewish "supreme court" of ancient times. It consisted of seventy sages.

Shabbos. Sabbath.

shishke (Yiddish). Pinecone.

shmittah. The sabbatical year. The Torah commands the farmer of the Land of Israel to let his land rest from agriculture every seven years. The fruit that grows on its own is holy and is subject to numerous restrictions. It is one of the tasks of the *kashrus* supervising authority to see to it that grapes used for wine in Israel are not prohibited by the laws of *shmittah*.

shul (Yiddish). Synagogue.

sugya (pl. *sugyos*). Talmudic topic(s).

terumos uma'asros. "Uplifted portions and tithes." Torah law stipulates that any produce grown in the Land of Israel is strictly forbidden until portions have been removed. In ancient times, it was donated to the Temple functionaries and the poor. Today the practice is different, but one of the functions of a *kashrus* supervising authority in Israel is to ensure that these "uplifted portions and tithes" are removed and processed properly.

Yasher koach. Congratulations! Well done!

yayin. Wine.

yeshivah bochur. Student in a religious/ rabbinical school.

WINE-PRODUCING REGIONS OF ISRAEL

Golan (or Golan Heights). A volcanic plateau overlooking the eastern side of the Sea of Galilee. A prime location for making wine, the Golan is considered part of the Galil "wine region."

Galil. The mountainous northern region of Israel. A prime area for Israeli wine making typified by high altitudes, marked temperature shifts between day and night, and rich, well-drained soils.

Shomron. A wine-growing region located in the northern part of the country not far from the seacoast. The Shomron includes the southern slopes of Mount Carmel. In the early days of Zionism, Baron Rothschild believed that this area was going to be a great wine-making region. He established the towns of Zichron Ya'akov and Binyamina as well as the Carmel wine company there. Over time, numerous wineries opened. Because the altitude is not very high in most places, the winters are humid and the summers are hot (with the exception of some areas high on the slopes of Mount Carmel). Because of this climate, the wineries of the Shomron often use grapes cultivated in the Galil or Golan for their better wines.

Shimshon. A wine-growing region located in the foothills of the Jerusalem Mountains and on the lower plains between the hills and the Tel Aviv area. This area is named for the biblical Samson, who was active there. The grapes grown there are not the best, most likely because of the mild winters and moist, humid summers in this region. (In general, noble grapes need sharp temperature changes between winter and summer and even between day and night to bring out their best qualities.) The wineries in this area almost always rely on grapes grown elsewhere for their fine wines.

Map labels: LEBANON, Metula, Nahariya, Akko, *Galilee*, Katzrin, *Golan Heights*, SYRIA, Haifa, Tzfat, Tiberias, *Sea of Galilee*, Nazareth, Afula, *Mt. Carmel*, Zikhron Ya'akov, *Jezreel Valley*, Binyamina, Beit She'an, *Shomron*, Netania, Nablus, Ariel, Tel Aviv, Rishon Le'Zion, Ashdod, Jericho, Jerusalem, Bethlehem, *Judaean Mountains*, *Shimshon*, Ashkelon, Hebron, *Dead Sea*, Beer Sheva, Dimona, Sde Boker, *The Negev*, JORDAN, Ramon, EGYPT

Legend:
- Winery
- Vineyard
- 0 25 50 Kilometers

Negev. The arid desert area of southern Israel. Until recently, the Negev was not considered a good place to grow grapes because of the low rainfall. However, there are many high-altitude areas with good soil conditions. Now that computerized drip irrigation technologies have become available, the Negev is emerging as a fine wine-producing area.

Harei Yehudah (Judean Hills). The mountainous area surrounding Jerusalem. This has been a prime wine region for millennia. There is a wide range of soil types here. The days are warm and the nights are cool due to the heightened elevation. This area is beginning to reassert itself as an excellent area for growing noble grape varieties.

Appendix 2
LINKS & RESOURCES

My interest in kosher wine expanded to the point that I felt compelled to create a website for like-minded individuals. I invite you to visit www.kosherwineclub.org for all things wine – information on kosher wine, wineries, and purchasing; updates; and more. Our website is ever-changing and it's a terrific way to keep track of what's new in the kosher wine world.

Below are some of the links you will find at the Kosher Wine Club. They are more elaborately explained on the site, so you may want to go there first to decide which ones to visit. In order to understand these links, here is information you should know about the wine industry. It will help you navigate the links with more savvy and a firmer sense of direction. (You may have seen some of this information in earlier chapters, but it bears repeating in this context.)

WHO'S WHO IN THE INDUSTRY

LIKE MANY businesses, the wine industry has three sides:

The Manufacturer: No matter what it is, somebody somewhere has to make it. Of course, wine is made by people who grow grapes, press them, and let the juice ferment. They are vintners and the places where they do their magic are called wineries. Some wineries are huge and make millions of bottles a year. Some are small, and make only a few thousand bottles a year. Being small gives you the ability to make something unique, so a lot of wine lovers get excited when they discover some new little operation. Every winery wants to move its product, and even a small winery will make too much wine to sell directly to the consumers. Imagine you made a few thousand bottles of wine, and now you have to wait for the shoppers to come and buy them. It will take ten years to sell one year's harvest! No one can survive that way. You need a distributor.

The Distributor: The distributor buys up lots of wine for a wholesale price. But how is he going to unload several million bottles of wine? He can't sell that much directly to consumers. So the distributor ships smaller amounts of wine to all the stores, the retailers. Distributors also make deals with wineries to help them promote and move their product.

The Retailer: The retailer receives a salable amount of wine. He puts it nicely on the shelves and hopes that somebody walks into the store to buy some. The retailer probably has the biggest challenge of all, because he has to convince customers (including the most educated consumer) to buy. As in any retail shop, the more he knows about the products he sells, the better he can sell them.

The manufacturer, distributor, and retailer all work together to bring you the wine you enjoy. Now, you might think up this sneaky idea: Why should I buy from the local retailer? Why don't I go straight to the winery? It will be much cheaper that way!

Your old Aunt Yenta might think this is a really clever idea. She might even pinch your cheek and call you a genius. The fact is that you can sometimes go to a winery's visitor center and do just that, but the vintner knows that it can't cut out the distributor. Even if he sells you and all your buddies a few bottles of wine, what is he going to do with the other thousands of bottles? The winery needs the distributor to survive. If he sells a few bottles at the winery, it doesn't hurt his relationship with the distributor. But to maintain that

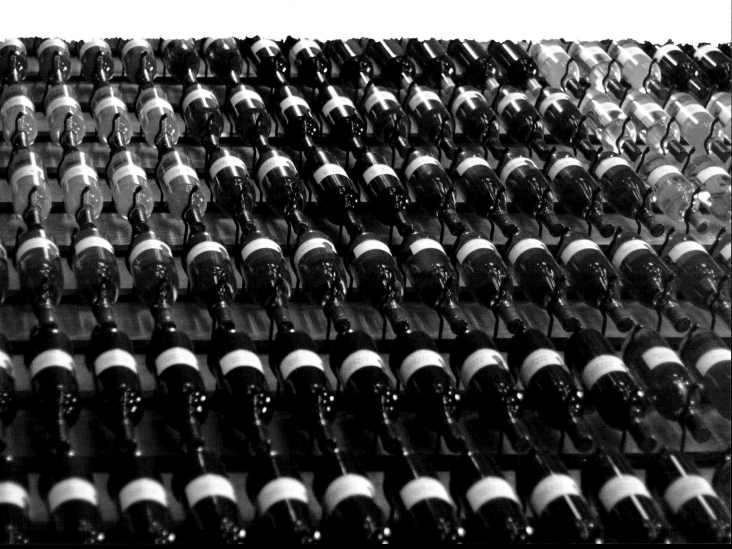

relationship, many wineries will not sell you anything over the Internet. Winery websites are primarily to inform you about what they do and to highlight their products, not to sell you wine.

The distributor won't sell you wine either. He is in the same position as the winery. He wants the retailers to survive and he won't cut them out. Distributors have websites where they show the different wines they buy from wineries all over the world. (Some wineries don't even have websites, because they rely on the distributor to advertise them.) The distributors' websites are entirely educational; you can look, but you can't buy wine there. If you happen to own a wine store, the distributor will happily sell wine to you, in bulk.

So you really have to go to the retailer. Believe me when I tell you, you need him and you want to be his friend. Tell your Aunt Yenta to look for bargains at the discount mall. You *want* to buy at your local wine store, especially if it specializes in kosher wine.

And here's why: the wine store guy remembers your name. He can help you with recommendations, give you tips, take care of all your quirky habits, place special orders for wines you like, and guide you as you try out new things. He will organize wine events and wine courses, and help make you into a connoisseur, instead of a wine-gulping *golem*. Be good to him. He works hard for his profit.

Still, some people live far from a kosher wine store, in which case you need links to online kosher wine stores, and to regular online wine stores with good kosher sections. These stores can ship worldwide.

Let me give you one really important tip. Wines need to settle down after being transported. Believe it or not, they get carsick and plane sick just like people. Whenever you get a wine in the mail, let it sit for at least forty-eight hours before you open it, to give time for the sediment to settle back down to the bottom of the bottle. Let it rest and it will be much happier in a day or two. You will be happier too.

As I suggested earlier, your best bet is to visit the online Kosher Wine Club in order to get your bearings and to enter the sites below as an informed consumer. But if you're ready, here are some shortcuts.

WINERIES

Wineries in Israel

Agur Winery
Moshav Agur 17
Emek Ha'Elah
Tel: 011-972-2-999-5423
Fax: 011-972-2-999-2088
yashuv@netvision.net.il
www.agurwines.com

Alexander Winery
POB 8151
Moshav Beit Yitzhak 42970
Tel: 011-972-2-991-0483
a_wine@netvision.net.il
www.alexander-winery.com

Arza Winery
POB 89, Adumim
industrial Park 98510
Tel: 011-972-2-535-1442
Fax: 011-972-2-2-5352128
office@arza.biz
www.arza.biz

Barkan Wine Cellars
POB 146, Kibbutz Hulda 76842
Tel: 011-972-8-935-5858
Fax: 011-972-8-935-5859
info@barkan-winery.co.il
Site: www.barkan-winery.co.il

Bazelet HaGolan
POB 77, Moshav Kidmat Zvi
Tel: 011-972-4-696-5010
Fax: 011-972-4-696-5020
bazelet@netvision.net.il
www.bazelet-hagolan.co.il

Ben Haim Winery
Moshav Gefen 99820
Tel: 011-972-3-676-2656
Fax: 011-972-3-574-1089
benhaim@benhaim.co.il
www.benhaim.co.il

Binyamina Wine Cellars
34 Hanassi St., Binyamina
Tel: 011-972-4-638-8643
Fax: 011-972-4-638-9021
shlomi@ben-hanna.com
www.binyaminawines.com

Bustan Winery
POB 55
Moshav Shaarei Tikva 44860
Cell: 011-972-54-489-2757
bustanwinery@yahoo.com

Carmel Winery – North
POB 2, Wine Street
Zichron Ya'akov 30950
Tel: 011-972-4-629-0977
Fax: 011-972-4-629-0957

Carmel Winery – South
POB 2, 25 Hacarmel St.
Rishon LeZion 75100
Tel: 011-972-3-948-8851
Fax: 011-972-3-966-3129
export@carmelwines.co.il
www.carmelwines.co.il

Dalton Winery
Dalton Industrial Park,
Merom HaGalil 13815
Tel: 011-972-4-698-7683
Fax: 011-972-4-698-7684
info@dalton-winery.com
www.dalton-winery.com

Domaine du Castel

Ramat Raziel, Upper Judea, 90974
Tel: 011-972-2-534-2249
Fax: 011-972-2-570-0995
castel@castel.co.il
www.castel.co.il

Ella Valley Vineyards

Kibbutz Netiv Halamed Heh
Tel: 011-972-2-999-4885
Fax: 011-972-4-999-4876
ella@ellavalley.com
www.ellavalley.com

Galil Mountain

Kibbutz Yiron
Tel: 011-972-4-686-8740
Fax: 011-972-4-686-8506
winery@galilmountain.co.il
www.galilmountain.co.il

Golan Heights Winery

POB 183, Katzrin Industrial Area
Tel: 011-972-4-696-8420
Fax: 011-972-4-696-2220
ghwinery@golanwines.co.il
www.golanwines.co.il

Gush Etzion Winery

POB 1415, Efrat 90435
Tel: 011-972-2-930-9220
Fax: 011-972-2-930-9156
winery@actcom.co.il
www.gushetzion-winery.com

Gvaot Winery

Givat Harel, Shiloh
Tel: 011-972-9-792-1292
Fax: 011-972-9-792-1086
amnonws@zahav.net.il
www.gvaot-winery.com

Hamasrek Winery

Moshav Beit Meir 90865
Tel: 011-972-2-570-1759
Fax: 011-972-2-533-6592
hamasrek@hamasrek.com
www.hamasrek.com

Kadesh Barnea Winery

Moshav Kadesh Barnea 85513
Tel: 011-972-8-655-5849
Fax: 011-972-8-655-8770
winerykb@012.net.il
www.kbw.co.il

Karmei Yosef

5 Erez St., Karmei Yosef
Cellular: 011-972-050-220-7022
Fax: 011-972-8-928-6118
hadar_n1@netvision.net.il
www.bravdo.com

Mony Winery

POB 275, Beit Shemesh 99000
Tel: 011-972-2-991-6629
Fax: 011-972-2-991-0366
monywines@walla.co.il

Noah/Hevron Heights Winery

Kiryat Arba Industrial Zone
Tel: 011-972-2-232-2251
Fax: 011-972-2-894-3006
directwine@012.net.il

Psagot Winery

Psagot 90624
Tel: 011-972-2-997-8222
Fax: 011-972-2-997-8222
bergpsagot@walla.com
www.psagotwines.com

Recanati Winery

Emek Hefer Industrial Zone
Tel: 011-972-4-622-2288
Fax: 011-972-4-622-8828
info@recanati-winery.com
www.recanati-winery.com

Rimon

Moshav Kerem Ben Zimra
Tel: 011-972-4-682-2325
Fax: 011-972-4-682-2324
info@rimonwinery.com
www.rimonwinery.com

Segal Wines

POB 140, Kibbutz Hulda
Tel: 011-972-8-935-8860
Fax: 011-972-8-935-8861
segal@segalwines.co.il
www.segalwines.co.il

Tabor Winery

POB 422, Kfar Tabor 15241
Tel: 011-972-4-676-0444
Fax: 011-972-4-677-2061
twc@twc.co.il
www.taborwinery.co.il

Tanya Winery

POB 422, Kfar Tabor 15241
Tel: 011-972-4-676-0444
Fax: 011-972-4-677-2061
tanyawinery@gmail.com
www.tanyawinery.co.il

Teperberg 1870

POB 609, Kibbutz Tzora 99803
Tel: 011-972-2-990-8080
Fax: 011-972-2-990-8090
service@teperberg1870.co.il
www.teperberg1870.co.il

Tishbi

Hameyasdim 33
Zichron Ya'akov
Tel: 011-972-4-638-0434/5
Fax: 011-972-4-638-0223
tishbi_w@netvision.net.il
www.tishbi.com

Tzora Vineyards

Kibutz Tzora
Tel: 011-972-2-990-8261
Fax: 011-972-2-991-5479
info@tzoravineyards.com
www.tzoravineyards.com

Tzuba Winery

Kibbutz Tzuba 90870
Tel: 011-972-2-534-7678
Fax: 011-972-2-534-7999
winery@tzuba.org.il
www.tzubawinery.co.il

Yatir Winery – Tel Arad

POB 5210, Arad
Tel: 011-972-8-995-9090
Fax: 011-972-8-995-9050
y_yatir@zahav.net.il
www.yatir.net

Zion Winery

45 Haruvit St.
Mishor Adumim Industrial Area
Tel: 011-972-2-535-2540
Fax: 011-972-2-535-5533
office@zionwines.co.il
http://zionfinewines.co.il/

European Kosher Wineries

Alaverdi Winery
Kakheti, Gurjaani Region, Georgia
Tel: 011-995-9-996-1222
info@alaverdi.ge
www.alaverdi.ge/eng/about.html

Alsace Wilmm Winery
32, rue du Docteur Sultzer
Barr, France 67140
Tel: 011-33-38-941-2431
Fax: 011-33-38-924-2054
contact@alsace-willm.com
http://alsace-willm.com/i_gb_nc.htm

Charles Guitard Vineyards
RN 113 Le recoude, 30670
Aigues-Vives, France
Tel: 011-33-46-651-7815
Fax: 011-33-46-671-5218
contact@vignoble-charlesguitard.fr
www.vignoble-charlesguitard.fr

Fortant Wines
info@fortant.com
www.fortant.com

HAFNER - Family Estate
Kosher & Organic Winery
Halbturner Str. 17 A-7123
Moenchhof, Austria
Tel: 011-43-21-738-0263
Fax.011-43 21-738-0689
julius.hafner@aon.at
www.kosher.at

Lambouri Winery (Yayin Kafrisin)
PO Box 59016, Platres
Limassol, Cyprus 4825
Tel: 011-357-2-542-2525
info@lambouri.com
www.kafrisin.com

New Zealand Kosher Wineries

Goose Bay Winery (Spencer Hill)
PO Box 3255, Richmond,
Nelson 7040 New Zealand
Tel: 011-64-3-543-2031
mail@spencerhillwine.com
www.spencerhillwine.com/

American Kosher Wineries

Four Gates Winery
Santa Cruz Mountains, CA
Tel: 1-831-457-2673
bc@fourgateswine.com
www.fourgateswine.com

Hagafen Cellars
4160 Silverado Trail
Napa, CA 94558
Tel: 1-888-HAGAFEN (424-2336)
info@hagafen.com
www.hagafen.com

Herzog Wine Cellars
3201 Camino Del Sol,
Oxnard, CA 93030
Tel: 1-805-983-1560
info@herzogwinecellars.com
www.herzogwinecellars.com

Manischewitz Wine Company
116 Buffalo Street,
Canandaigua, NY 14424
Tel: 1-585-374-6311
www.manischewitzwine.com

Red Fern Cellars
POB 706, Lawrence, NY 11559
sales@redferncellars.com
www.redferncellars.com

Photo:
Ofir Gardi

WINE DISTRIBUTORS

These companies buy kosher wines from all over the world. If you want to find out what is kosher in the classic French wineries, Italian wineries – or anywhere in the world – these links will tell you what is out there.

Abarbanel Wine Co.
100 Cedarhurst Ave., Cedarhurst, NY
mail@admiralimports.com
www.kosher-wine.com

Royal Wine Corp.
63 LeFante Lane, Bayonne, NJ 07002
Tel: 1-718-384-2400
customerservice@royalwines.com
www.royalwines.com

Welner International Kosher Wine Producers
1 Yetziat Europa Street, Herzliya, Israel
Tel: 011-972-9-958-5485/6
Fax: 011-972-3-725-6336
info@welnerwines.com
www.welnerwines.com

ONLINE WINE STORES

If you live far, far from any kosher wine store, first let me congratulate you on deciding to seek out a kosher wine. You will need these links to get your wine.

Buy Wine
www.BuyWine.co.il

The Jerusalem Wine Store
www.myisraeliwine.com

Kosher Wine
www.kosherwine.com

The Kosher Wine Outlet
www.kosherwineoutlet.com

The Kosher Wine Rack
www.kosherwinerack.com

My Kosher Wine
www.mykosherwine.com

Online Kosher Wine
www.onlinekosherwine.com

Only Kosher Wine
www.onlykosherwine.com

Kadesh Barnea

WINE INFO SITES

These are sites you can go to for more information, or to read other people's opinions about the wines they've tried. Daniel Rogov, z"l, who wrote the introduction to this book, was one of the best wine "raters" around. His objectivity was very special. He would do wine tastings without seeing the bottles, so he rated the wines without knowing what they were. Then he retasted, and if he found that he gave a wine two different scores, he would throw away all his notes from that tasting, take a day off to straighten out his taste buds, and do it all over again. You can still find his reviews online and in his final, 2011 edition of *Rogov's Guides to Israeli and World Kosher Wines*. You don't have to agree with Rogov's reviews or anyone else's. Taste is personal.

The Grapevine, a store in Wesley Hills (Monsey), New York, owned and operated by Yoel Smith, provides online video wine reviews. The Grapevine staff was very helpful in the research for this book. Store manager Yehoshua Werth hosts the highly informative wine-tasting reviews. You can find the reviews by going to the store website: *www.thegrapevinewines.com*.

The Grapevine
http://blog.herzogwinecellars.com

The Kosher Sommelier
www.koshersommelier.blogspot.com

Kosher Wine Report
www.yossiescorkboard.com

Kosher Wine Society
www.kosherwinesociety.com

My Kerem
www.mykerem.com

Wine Library TV
http://tv.winelibrary.com/

Wine Lovers Discussion Group
www.wineloverspage.com

Kosher Wine Club
www.kosherwineclub.com

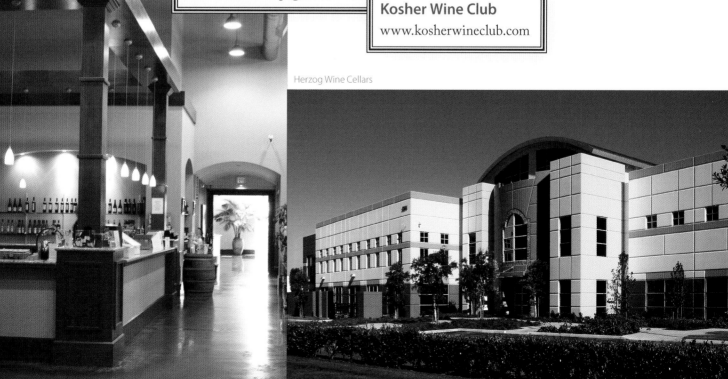

Herzog Wine Cellars